ISBN 978-1-943521-54-8

Boyack, Connor, author.
Stanfield, Elijah, illustrator.
Hague, Katie Phipps, editor.
The Tuttle Twins Guide to Courageous Heroes / Connor Boyack.

Cover design by Elijah Stanfield
Edited and typeset by Connor Boyack

Printed in the United States

10 9 8 7 6 5 4 3 2 1

THE TUTTLE TWINS GUIDE TO
COURAGEOUS HEROES

BY CONNOR BOYACK

The List of HEROES

You know what part of history we don't like? It's all the examples there are of countless people supporting really awful things. In countries throughout the world, many people have quietly tolerated or loudly supported bad politicians and policies that hurt people.

Our parents have taught us since we were young that we should stand up for what is right—even if other people disagree. That takes courage, obviously. And sometimes it can even be dangerous.

That's why we've loved learning about stories of other people who have been courageous. These stories are exciting and inspiring, and they help us think about how we might act if we were ever in similar circumstances.

Have you ever thought about that? Imagine that your family and friends were all supporting a law that treated people of a different religion or race poorly—taking their property or throwing them in jail. What would you do if you believed differently? How might you find the courage to speak out in favor of truth?

Whatever the issue might be, there are many evils in our world that people like you and us should speak out against. That's intimidating for many people, but we still think it's important to choose what is right, and let the consequence follow. That's why it's fun for us to learn from the stories of other courageous people who lived before us.

Maybe one day you'll find yourself in a situation where you have to do something bold and even controversial in order to stand up for what's right.

Hopefully the stories we'll be sharing with you in this book will help motivate you to make the right decision when that day comes.

Take the time to really get into these stories and think about how their example can inspire you!

Even better, share these stories with your siblings, parents, and friends so they can learn as well.

In the near future we're probably going to need many more heroes to do what is right!

—The Tuttle Twins

Corrie
ten Boom

Standing true to their faith and love of humanity, the ten Boom family defied the orders of the occupying government. Many of them accepted torture and death rather than betray their conscience, but Corrie survived and her convictions inspire us today.

A Tiny Baby with a Very Big Name

In the early morning of April 15, 1892, a tiny little girl arrived a month earlier than expected to a small, love-filled home in Amsterdam, Netherlands.

Her uncle, upon seeing her skinny little newborn body, remarked that it would probably be best if the Lord quickly took the child to Heaven because he feared she would never have much of a future, considering her frail and unhealthy start. Maybe it was because her parents gave her such a big name, or maybe it was because Cornelia Arnolda Johanna ten Boom had such important work to do, but the Lord did not take Cornelia up to Heaven—not then, and not for a very, very long time afterward.

When Corrie, as she was called, was five, her grandfather died, leaving the ten Boom clock shop to her father. Corrie, along with her parents and older siblings, Elizabeth (Betsie), Willem, and Nollie, left Amsterdam for the quaint town of Haarlem. The ten Boom clock shop had already been in the family for nearly a hundred years by the time Corrie and her family took up residence within its oddly shaped rooms connected by winding hallways and twisted staircases. Renovation after renovation had left its floors misaligned and its walls uneven, but the ten Boom family never seemed to mind. They were known for always making the best of everything they had and for always creating a loving and welcoming home environment for their own family, as well as all whom they would welcome as family throughout the years.

Corrie loved to study and was always seeking ways to improve herself and help those around her. By the time she reached adulthood, she was fluent in Dutch, English,

German, and French. She even spoke a little Hebrew and Greek! Corrie was known for her beautiful singing voice, and she loved to gather with her family to sing songs together while her nephew, Peter, played the piano or the organ. By the time her mother died in 1921, Corrie had joined her father as a watchmaker. In fact, Corrie was the first licensed female watchmaker in all of Holland!

Corrie was 29, and although some of her siblings were married with families, Corrie and her oldest sister, Betsie, remained single. Later in her life, Corrie would tell of a young man whom she loved and who she thought loved her. She thought that he would propose marriage to her and was left heartbroken when the relationship came to an end. Her father took his daughter's face gently in his hands and said, "Corrie, what you are feeling is love. Sometimes we love something or someone so much that it can cause us to feel a lot of pain. You have two choices right now. You can choose to turn off that love—to banish it away so that you don't feel the pain that it has caused—or you can choose to find ways to turn that love toward something else." Corrie listened to her father, and although she never did marry, she spent her life finding places to use all the love that she had inside her—even when it hurt.

With the help of her sister Betsie, Corrie organized a youth club for teenage girls. When she wasn't working as a watchmaker, she and Betsie spent their time giving religious instruction and sewing lessons, teaching the performing arts (the ten Boom family loved to practice and perform plays), and providing friendship and camaraderie to the dozens of young girls who joined their club. The ten Booms were devout members of the Dutch Reformed

Church and believed that it was their honor and duty to spend their time in service to their fellowman and attending to those less fortunate. The crooked walls of the ten Boom home were never closed to those needing food or shelter, and although they never had children of their own, Betsie and Corrie fostered seventeen children throughout their lives and saved countless families from homelessness and starvation.

A Shadow Falls

On the 10th of May, 1940, Germany and Hitler's Nazis invaded Holland. The Dutch army fought valiantly against the Nazi advance, but within four days, Queen Wilhelmina had fled to London, and the army had fallen. Holland was now a German-occupied nation.

And occupy they did. The first thing the Nazis did was gather able-bodied Dutch men and force them to sign oaths of allegiance to Germany if they wanted to be able to continue to work. If they refused to sign, they would have to go into hiding in order to avoid being arrested and sent away to labor camps. Many who signed became what the Dutch called "collaborators." Collaborators were men who provided information to the Nazis about other Dutch people in exchange for extra food-ration cards, extra pay at their jobs, and extra privileges. These traitors were very dangerous, because no one knew who they were. Dutch families who still loved their queen and their country and who despised the Nazi occupiers had to hide their thoughts and their feelings from their neighbors, because they never knew when someone might be spying on them in order to turn them in. People began to live in fear and suspicion.

But Corrie and the rest of the ten Boom family didn't live in fear. They had their faith and their strong sense of right and wrong, and they knew what they had to do. By 1941, Corrie and Betsie had started an underground operation to help people who were being persecuted by the Nazis to hide or escape. And who were the Nazis persecuting? Sometimes it seemed like everyone, but there was one group of people who were particularly hated by Adolf Hitler and his followers.

In his book, *Mein Kampf*, the Nazi leader wrote that the "Jew is like a vampire; for wherever he establishes himself the people who grant him hospitality are bound to be bled to death sooner or later." Hitler believed that the Jews were a threat to his country and his people, and he convinced many people that he was right by using propaganda to make people afraid or distrustful of Jewish people. He made a plan and called it "The Final Solution." He intended to use his power and his army to kill or remove every single Jew from all of Europe.

Not everyone agreed with Hitler, but a lot of people did. Even in Holland, not many Dutchmen spoke up when the Nazis issued ID cards that everyone had to keep on them at all times. Hardly anyone spoke up when they realized that people of Jewish heritage, even their friends and neighbors, had a very large and prominent "J" on their cards. By May of 1942, two years into the German occupation, Jews were forced to sew a yellow Star of David with the word Jude (Jew) in the center onto all of their clothing. Now Jews were able to be picked out of any crowd on any street. Dutch restaurants stopped serving Jews. People stopped visiting Jewish shops, and German police seemed to always be close by, harassing Jewish people, young and old alike. Everyone began noticing Jewish families being rounded up in the middle of the night and taken to the train station. Whispers spread that they were being taken to labor camps to help the Germans make supplies for the war. Some whispers told of something much more sinister than labor camps, but not many people believed those things could be true.

Some people, like Corrie's nephew Peter, found ways to help Dutchmen remember who they were and remember their lives before occupation. On May 10, 1942, on the two-year anniversary of the German invasion, Peter was playing the organ at church. When the congregation rose to sing the final hymn, Peter played the first few notes of the Dutch National Anthem. Slowly, he played on, and one voice, and then two, and then dozens joined in as he played with all his heart. By the time Peter was taken away by the Nazis, the whole congregation had joined in a rousing rendition of their country's anthem. Small acts of courage and defiance—like Peter's—sprang up here and there, but punishment was always harsh and swift, and the threat of prison and labor camps did much to keep most people quiet and obedient to their occupiers.

But not the ten Booms. They were still not afraid to do what was right. By 1943, Corrie and her sister had anywhere between seven and twelve Jews hiding in their home at all times. Their father, who was by then a very old man, supported his daughters in their efforts and did all that he could to protect and provide for their frightened houseguests. As time went on, people began to notice extra activity around the watchmakers' house. The ten Booms knew that trouble was coming. Corrie devised a system of bells and buzzers to alert everyone in the house when there was someone at the door. She had a trusted friend—an architect—come in and build a very small room behind a double brick wall in her bedroom. Everyone in the house would hold drills where they would pretend that the Nazis were at the door, and they would hide their guests in the tiny, hidden room and rehearse what they would say if they were interrogated.

On February 28th, 1944, Corrie was laying down in her bed, sick with a fever. Her family was downstairs holding their weekly Bible study, when she heard the buzzers and bells begin to sound. In her feverish state she thought, "I don't remember planning a drill for today?" But when her Jewish friends rushed into her bedroom with terror in their eyes and pushed aside her wardrobe to reveal the hiding place behind the double brick, Corrie knew that this was not a drill. Just as she slipped the wardrobe back into place, Nazi officers entered her room, grabbing her roughly and yelling at her to reveal where she was harboring the Jews. Corrie was 52 years old.

Arrest and Imprisonment

The Nazi officers severely beat Betsie and Corrie, but no one in the house revealed the hidden Jews. Corrie, Betsie, and their 85-year-old father were arrested and taken to prison. Before loading Casper up in the truck, a Nazi officer who felt compassion for the old man said, "If you can tell me you will behave, you can die at home in your own bed like you have earned the right to do." Casper replied, "If you leave me here today, tomorrow I will open my door to whoever needs help."

Casper ten Boom died in prison on May 9, 1944. He was buried in an unmarked grave.

Shortly after their father's death, Betsie and Corrie were reunited when they were transferred to Herzogenbusch, a women's labor camp in Holland. Corrie told her sister that while in prison, a message had been smuggled to her, "All watches in your closet are safe," it had read. Despite the arrest of the ten Boom family, none of the Jews had been found, and all had safely escaped to other safe-houses.

Three months after arriving at Herzogenbusch, Corrie and Betsie were loaded up into train cars meant for transporting cattle. There wasn't even room for them to sit down, and there was no protection from the elements. Three days later, they arrived at the Ravensbrück concentration camp deep inside Germany. 35,000 women were housed at Ravensbrück with 1,400 women living in barracks designed for only 400. The barracks were overrun with rodents and disease-carrying bugs, but Corrie later remarked that she counted the living conditions as a blessing because they kept the guards from coming too close, and the women were able to hold two Bible studies a day, where Corrie and Betsie taught from a Bible that Corrie had managed to smuggle into the camp.

Life at Ravensbrück was brutal. One day, a guard became frustrated with Betsie because she worked too slowly. She was sixty years old and unable to carry the weight of the tasks assigned to her. The guard beat her severely, and she was taken to the crude camp hospital to recover from her injuries. A nurse tasked with caring for Betsie was cruel to her, and Corrie struggled to not let hatred fill her heart and chase out all the love she had once held. Betsie reminded her to forgive, and Corrie was once again strengthened by her older sister's faith and wise counsel.

Betsie died just three months after arriving at Ravens-brück. She never did recover from the beating. Corrie was able to see her sister one last time before she was buried at the camp and later recounted, "I saw joy and peace on her face. She even looked young." Corrie knew that her sister had died as she had lived—full of love and gratitude for her God and compassion for her fellowman.

A few days later, while in line for the morning roll call, Corrie's prisoner number was called. "6-6-7-3-0," said the guard. Corrie stepped forward. She thought that she was going to be killed. But something else happened. She was taken to the prison office and told that she was free to go. She was being released!

Later, Corrie found out that her number had been called by mistake. There had been a clerical error in the office that day, and her number had accidently been included with those who were to be set free. Later, she also learned that a week after she left, all the women at Ravensbrück who were her age or older had been executed. New prisoners were arriving, and the Nazis had decided to kill the old and weak to make room for younger, more valuable workers.

I Dared to Be Happy!

Corrie returned to the crooked old clock shop on the corner, but everything had changed. Her family was gone. She was all alone now. She could have been very sad. She could have been bitter. Her family had suffered so much. She had suffered so much! But bitterness and anger never was the ten Boom way, and it wasn't going to start being their way now. Corrie remembered the dreams Betsie had shared with her inside the dark walls of Ravensbrück. Even in the midst of so much suffering, Betsie was planning trips for Corrie, telling her all the places she must visit and all the people she could help by sharing their story.

And that's what Corrie did. She spent the rest of her life visiting countries all over the world and writing books, sharing her stories and her messages of love and compassion and forgiveness and selfless service to others.

Once, a man approached her after she finished speaking. He was old and stooped, and his head was bent down in shame. "I was a guard at Ravensbrück," he said. "I was there at the same time as you and your sister." Corrie's heart broke. How could she forgive this man? She closed her eyes and said a silent prayer: "God, I can lift my hand, if you supply the feelings." She opened her eyes and lifted her hand, placing it in the outstretched hand of the Nazi guard. She felt peace, and when she met his tear-filled eyes, she said, "I forgive you with all my heart."

And she meant it.

Corrie lived to forgive other Nazi guards who sought her out to make their peace. She even forgave the nurse who had treated her beloved sister so cruelly as she lay suffering in her hospital bed.

It is estimated that more than 800 Jews were saved by Corrie and her underground network.

Cornelia Arnolda Johanna ten Boom died in Placentia, California, on April 15, 1983. It was her 91st birthday.

Harriet
TUBMAN

One of the most iconic heroes in history, Harriet Tubman dedicated her life to freeing slaves and guiding them through dangerous territory using a secret network of hiding places known as the "Underground Railroad."

A Tough Beginning

Harriet Tubman stood in the corner of the dimly lit room. Whenever her master flew into a rage at one of his slaves, Harriet tried to be as far away from him as possible, but tonight she had nowhere to go. She didn't want to draw his attention or anger by running out of the room, so she tried instead to hold as still as could and tuck herself as far into the corner as possible.

She never did learn what object her master had picked up, but she saw its heavy darkness in his hand as he drew back and let the thing fly. She closed her eyes, anticipating the sickening thud that always accompanied such a mighty blow, but instead she felt white-hot pain in her head. A slow moment passed as she tried to make sense of the darkness closing in around her. Then she slumped to the floor, and all went black.

Someone moved her to a bench, and there she lay for two days, bleeding from the head and drifting in and out of consciousness. Harriet was ten years old.

She would later speak of the traumatizing experience: "The weight broke my skull…. They carried me to the house all bleeding and fainting. I had no bed, no place to lie down on at all, and they laid me down on the seat of the loom and I stayed there all day and the next."

Harriet Tubman was born in 1820 on a plantation in Maryland. Her parents, Harriet "Rit" Green and Benjamin Ross, named her Araminta Ross and referred to her fondly as "Minty." Araminta would later change her name to Harriet in tribute to her mother. She had eight siblings, but despite her mother's desperate efforts to keep all of her children together and with her, a slave had no right to own anything—even her own children—and Harriet and her siblings were often separated from the rest of the family.

The first time Harriet was taken away, she was only five years old. She was assigned to work as a nurse for her master's baby and was in charge of feeding, cleaning, rocking, and all general care of the infant. It was very hard for such a small child to take care of a baby, but her master wasn't a gentle person and didn't seem to care that what he expected of the little girl was nearly impossible. The life of a slave was often harsh, and physical punishment was commonly used to discourage "disobedience" or "poor performance." Harriet suffered beatings if the baby in her care was too fussy, or if he woke up too soon from his naps. Harriet was barely more than a baby herself, yet she was charged with the care of someone else's child and punished severely if she didn't perform her tasks to her master's liking.

Harriet would bear the scars from her childhood beatings her whole life.

At seven years old, Harriet was sent to work on a plantation several miles away. It was here that she was put to work in the fields for the first time and here that she determined that she would rather do hard, manual labor in the sweltering heat or bitter cold than be charged with indoor, domestic chores. At least when she worked with her hands and the strength of her own body, she was in control of how well she accomplished her task. Here, at least, she was no longer at the mercy of an inconsolable infant, and in the fields she was out of reach of her quick-tempered master.

Sometimes, a slave owner freed his slaves upon his death, and this was the case for Harriet and her family. Unfortunately, the people who inherited a plantation were sometimes dishonest, and this was the case for Harriet and her family as well. Harriet had spent the first twenty years of her life as a slave—her mother had spent even longer—but although her mother and siblings had been freed in their master's will, the new owners of the plantation refused to acknowledge their freedom. They remained enslaved. Harriet's father, Benjamin, was eventually freed, but he chose to stay with his family.

The Underground Railroad

When she was 24, Harriet married a man named John Tubman. John was a free black man, but he wasn't very kind. He would often fly into fits of temper and threaten to sell Harriet, who was, in a way, doubly enslaved—owned by her master, and also by her husband who seemed to delight in her hardships and suffering. Finally, Harriet could bear no more.

She resolved to escape her slavery.

One cold morning, twenty-six-year-old Harriet Tubman left her husband and her family and fled north along a route called the Underground Railroad. Her escape took several days, but she eventually arrived in Philadelphia where she found work as a housekeeper. She was free!

But the sweetness of freedom quickly lost its savor. Harriet struggled to find happiness as a free woman knowing her family and loved ones were still in bondage. She decided to go back to Maryland, braving the risk of capture and the perilous journey, in order to free as many of her loved ones as she could. She was able to secure her niece and her niece's daughter, and once again she traveled the Underground Railroad back to Pennsylvania and freedom.

Later that year, Congress passed the Fugitive Slave Act, making it legal for slave owners to reclaim slaves who had escaped to the north. Rewards were offered for the return of slaves. Suddenly, even living in Philadelphia wasn't safe.

But the Fugitive Slave Act didn't stop Harriet from working to free those still in bondage. Those who couldn't leave with her were given detailed instructions, including safehouses, routes according to time of year and weather, and the names of fellow abolitionists who could be counted on to help. Harriet was known to take those she had rescued as far north as Canada to ensure that they wouldn't be captured by those looking to collect rewards for runaway slaves.

By the time she was forty, she had run the Underground Railroad 19 times and had freed over 300 slaves. Later she recalled, "I never ran my train off the track and I never lost a passenger."

War!

When Harriet was forty-one years old, the war between the states broke out, and she found new ways to free enslaved people. She began working for the north, or the Union, as a soldier and spy. Her years of travel on the Underground Railroad had given her a keen sense of direction, the ability to handle a weapon with ease, and the skill of moving silently through heavily wooded areas. She became the first woman to ever lead a military operation in the United States.

At the beginning of the war, Harriet thought that President Lincoln should free the slaves in the south, but he was unwilling at the time to do so. She took him to task when she wrote,

> God won't let master Lincoln beat the South till he does *the right thing*. Master Lincoln, he's a great man, and I am a poor negro; but the negro can tell master Lincoln how to save the money and the young men. He can do it by setting the negro free. Suppose that was an awful big snake down there, on the floor. He bite you. Folks all scared, because you die. You send for a doctor to cut the bite; but the snake, he rolled up there, and while the doctor doing it, he bite you *again*. The doctor dug out *that* bite; but while the doctor doing it, the snake, he spring up and bite you again; so he *keep* doing it, till you kill *him*. That's what master Lincoln ought to know.

Eventually, President Lincoln did support emancipation, but Harriet never did forget his unwillingness to make it a priority from the start.

Despite her contribution to the Union cause, Harriet was never paid regular wages and was denied her pension after the war ended. She spent all of her time and money helping those less fortunate than herself and often suffered great poverty and personal hardship because of her generosity. She worked odd jobs and took in boarders to help pay her bills and care for her aging parents.

One of the boarders she cared for was a man named Nelson Charles Davis. He was 22 years younger than Harriet, but they soon fell in love and were married in 1869. Although she never had children of her own, Nelson and Harriet adopted a baby girl in 1874. They named her Gertie and lived together as a happy family until Nelson's death in 1888.

Finally, at the end of her life, the U.S. government finally began righting some of the financial wrongs Harriet had suffered because of their unwillingness to pay her wages and her pension. At the age of 75, Harriet began receiving the pension she had earned for her service as a soldier and spy during the Civil War. Never one to think of herself, she used her pension to open the Harriet Tubman Home for the Aged, a home where the elderly could receive care and comfort whether or not they could afford to pay.

The famous abolitionist Frederick Douglass wrote a letter to Harriet that perfectly captured the humility and selfless-ness with which she lived her life. He said,

> Dear Harriet: I am glad to know that the story of your eventful life has been written by a kind lady, and that the same is soon to be published. You ask for what you do not need when you call upon me for a word of commendation. I need such words from you far more than you can need them from me, especially where your superior labors and devotion to the cause of the lately enslaved of our land are known as I know them.
>
> The difference between us is very marked. Most that I

have done and suffered in the service of our cause has been in public, and I have received much encouragement at every step of the way. You, on the other hand, have labored in a private way. I have wrought in the day – you in the night. I have had the applause of the crowd and the satisfaction that comes of being approved by the multitude, while the most that you have done has been witnessed by a few trembling, scarred, and foot-sore bondmen and women, whom you have led out of the house of bondage, and whose heartfelt, "God bless you," has been your only reward.

The midnight sky and the silent stars have been the witnesses of your devotion to freedom and of your heroism. Excepting John Brown – of sacred memory – I know of no one who has willingly encountered more perils and hardships to serve our enslaved people than you have. Much that you have done would seem improbable to those who do not know you as I know you. It is to me a great pleasure and a great privilege to bear testimony for your character and your works, and to say to those to whom you may come, that I regard you in every way truthful and trustworthy.

Your friend,

Frederick Douglass

Harriet died in 1913 at the age of 91. She had hardly any earthly possessions, and barely a penny to her name. Living at the time as a guest at the Harriet Tubman Home for the Aged, she was surrounded by friends and family and told them just before she passed, "I go to prepare a place for you."

Booker T.
WASHINGTON

Soldiers from the northern states freed
young Booker from slavery, but he spent
the rest of his life trying to free his peers
from the persecution they still lived under.
His strategy? Provide opportunities for
black people to become the best educated and most industrious Americans.

From Slave Shack to the White House

On April 5th, 1856, in a shack in Hale's Ford, Virginia, a scholar was born. At the time, of course, he appeared to be a very average baby. He had an average face and an average head of thick, soft, curly hair. He had an average cry, and an average temperament. Nothing particularly interesting or noteworthy accompanied his birth or his early life. His mother was a slave, so upon his birth he became a slave as well—the human property of the master of the house. His mother was a cook.

But sometimes, the very greatest of people are born into the most average of circumstances, and Booker T. Washington was indeed destined for greatness.

When Booker was nine, the Great War ended, and his master and mistress set him and his mother, sister, and brother free. The small family moved to Malden, West Virginia, where his mother, Jane, soon met and married a man named Washington Ferguson—a free black man. Booker and his siblings finally had a father, and his family set out to build a life for themselves.

In Malden, even though he was still very young, Booker was responsible for helping to contribute to his family's finances. He worked each morning in a local salt mine from 4-9 AM. When the bell rang, he rushed home for breakfast, changed out of his dirty clothes, and ran out the door to school. Booker loved learning, and having experienced life without the freedom to attend school, he now relished every moment he could spend in his studies. After school, he quickly ate again and set out for his second job, where he worked in a coal mine.

The work was hard, and often his lungs ached because of the fine coal dust that hung thick in the air, but Booker didn't mind. He liked the way it felt to collect his paycheck and take it home to his mother and father. When he sat down at the table, he felt proud that his hard work helped purchase the good food his family had to eat. He loved the ownership that he and his loved ones had over their own lives—he felt like the whole world was open to him and that all that stood between him and any dream he could imagine was hard work.

One day, while working in the mines, he overheard someone talking about a place called the Hampton Institute—a school for former slaves founded by Brigadier General Samuel Chapman Armstrong, who had led the 9th United States Colored Infantry during the Civil War. Armstrong had been troubled by the lack of educational opportunities available to blacks in the United States, so even as the war raged on, he laid the foundation for a school to educate and empower them. When the war ended, Armstrong dedicated the rest of his life to this cause.

Booker was determined to further his education and opportunities at the Hampton Institute and was undeterred by the fact that it was 500 miles away.

Early in the morning, on a day that was not particularly remarkable, Booker Washington rose early and gathered with his family for goodbye hugs and kisses and one last family prayer. His mother and father stood at the door and waved goodbye as their son set out on his journey. He had no money for a carriage ride, but he didn't mind. He figured he had two perfectly good feet and a nice, strong back, so Booker T. walked the 500 miles to Hampton Institute.

The year was 1872, and Booker was sixteen.

He graduated from Hampton in 1875 and returned to Malden to teach. He loved teaching and always combined his belief in hard work and a strong moral character into every lesson he taught. In Malden, he educated the city's children by day, and at night he taught adults—poor men and women, free black men, former slaves, and anyone else who wanted to put in the work to make themselves more than they currently were.

In 1879, General Amrstrong, impressed by the hard work and stalwart character Washington showed during his time at Hampton, recommended him as principal for a brand new school that was opening in Tuskegee, Alabama.

And so, Booker said goodbye to his family again and headed south.

The Atlanta Compromise

Booker fit right in at the Tuskegee Normal and Industrial Institute. He would spend the rest of his life building the school and using his resources to empower and educate black men and women, as well as others who lacked the opportunities afforded to more affluent members of society.

The post-Reconstruction era in the south made life hard for black people. "Jim Crow" laws, which legalized the segregation of whites and blacks, made it difficult for black people to find good jobs and often barred them from gaining any type of meaningful education. The Ku Klux Klan, a racist organization that opposed integration of black people into white society, was becoming more powerful—and more violent.

Washington recognized the danger blacks faced as they tried to get ahead in life. He determined that it would be a waste of time and effort for black people to make the fight for equality their focus—he knew that hate-filled people could not be reasoned with, and he didn't want to see his people get dragged into a losing battle where they would surely be the ones to suffer. Instead, Washington believed that white people could have their "black-free" society. He believed that, rather than force bigoted people to live and work with those they were determined to hate, black people should put their time and efforts into bettering themselves.

In a famous speech that would become known as The Atlanta Compromise, he told a white audience that he thought segregation was fine, but that black people should be granted the same access to the economy, education, and equality under law as white people. He argued that blacks didn't need white politicians to give them a leg up or to force other whites to accept them. He instead advocated for blacks to focus on becoming well-educated, learning valuable and marketable skills and trades, owning their own land and businesses, and building personal wealth. He argued that acquiring wealth, property, and education would do more to put black people on equal standing with whites than any amount of legislation ever would.

He admonished people to remember that,

> The wisest of my race understand that the agitation
> of questions of social equality is the extremest folly

and that progress in the enjoyment of all the privileges that will come to us must be the result of severe and constant struggle rather than artificial forcing. The opportunity to earn a dollar in a factory just now is worth infinitely more than to spend a dollar in an opera house.

Booker T. Washington didn't want whites to grant blacks the privilege of attending the opera; he wanted blacks to open opera houses that whites would pay them to attend. He wanted true progress and empowerment—not conditional empowerment granted out of charity or pity.

W.E.B. Dubois

Washington believed that in order to compete as true equals with whites, black people would need to become independent and successful without the help of others. He saw what he viewed as a troubling pattern in some members of the black community to put all of their focus on forcing equality and social justice and getting whites to acknowledge and fix all of the wrongs that had been committed against them. He said,

> There is another class of coloured people who make a business of keeping the troubles, the wrongs, and the hardships of the Negro race before the public. Having learned that they are able to make a living out of their troubles, they have grown into the settled habit of advertising their wrongs—partly because they want sympathy and partly because it pays. Some of these people do not want the Negro to lose his grievances, because they do not want to lose their jobs.

One of these people was a man named W.E.B. Dubois.

Dubois was born in 1868, three years after the end of the Civil War. He was raised in Great Barrington, Massachusetts, in an integrated town with a large population of free blacks. He attended a mixed-race school where he had both black and white friends. His teachers recognized his intelligence and encouraged him to pursue his studies with vigor. He graduated from Great Barrington's Searles High School near the top of his class and, after graduation, decided he wanted to go on to college. His childhood congregation at the First Congregational Church of Great Barrington raised the money to send him.

He attended Fisk University in Nashville, Tennessee, and graduated in 1888 with his bachelor's degree. His church continued to pay his tuition through his years at Fisk, and in 1888, he enrolled at Harvard College and began work on a second bachelor's degree. This time, he paid his tuition with money from summer jobs, an inheritance, scholarships, and loans from friends. In 1890, he received his bachelor's degree in history from Harvard and, in 1891, was offered a scholarship to attend their sociology graduate school. He spent three years studying and completing graduate research across Europe, spending a significant amount of time in Germany, where, through the influence of prominent economists and sociologists of the time, he became a Socialist—a political affiliation he would hold for the rest of his life.

He returned to the United States and, in 1895, became the first black man to earn a PhD from Harvard University.

Although Dubois initially supported Washington's Atlanta Compromise, he soon turned away from it, believing instead that blacks should put all of their efforts into gaining equal treatment and social justice for the wrongs they had suffered. Dubois and Washington remained at odds in their vision for how best to usher in equality and racial harmony between blacks and whites. Washington would found the National Negro Business League, and Dubois would found the National Association for the Advancement of Colored People (NAACP).

Many in the black community agreed with Dubois and believed that the top priority should be pursuing full civil rights for all, but Washington disagreed, saying, "In all things that are purely social we can be separate as the fingers, yet one as the hand in all things essential to mutual progress." While there were many who did not agree with Washington, there were others who liked his way of thinking—they found it empowering.

Washington believed that more influence among white people could be gained through business ties than through political channels. He understood that businessmen could find common ground and respect for one another in ways that others could not, and he fostered these relationships in his own life, forming alliances with wealthy and powerful whites. He used these ties to influence philanthropists to donate to black organizations and businesses that he saw as deserving of help and promotion.

As time went on and criticism from Dubois and his followers mounted, Washington attempted to clarify some of his beliefs in a letter to the editor of the *Birmingham Age-Herald*:

Tuskegee, Alabama

November 24, 1902

I notice that several newspapers have recently connected my name with political matters in such a manner as to show that my position is misunderstood. I desire, therefore, to make the following statement:

My life work is the promotion of the education of my race. It is well known that I have always advised my people that it is of supreme importance, at this period of their development, that should concentrate their thought and energy on the securing of homes, the cultivation of habits of thrift, economy, skill, intelligence, high moral character, and the gaining of the respect and confidence of their neighbors, white and black, both in the south and in the north. From such teaching and counsel, no influence can ever divert me. Whatever conferences I have had with the President or with any public official have grown out of my position, not as a politician, but as an educator.

It should be borne in mind that there are about nine millions of negroes in the United States, who are liable under the law for taxes and military service, and who are punishable for infraction of the law. These people at present have no member of their race in the national law-making body, and it is right that those charged with making and executing the laws of the land should at times seek information directly from members of the negro race when their interests and their relations with the whites among whom they live are concerned. Under no circumstances could I seek to promote political candidacies or volunteer information regarding men or measures, nor have I done so in the past; but because of the importance I have always sought to place upon education and industry among my people as the bases of friendly relations between the races, there may be occasions in the future as there have been in the past, when, if I am so requested, I can give information about men and measures, which would tend to promote such friendly relations between the races, such information it is my duty to give when it is asked for.

At every proper opportunity I say to the youth of our people that they will make a mistake if they seek to succeed in life by mere political activity or the hope of holding political office. Now and then, however, public questions affecting our interests arise which are so fundamental and far-reaching that they transcend the domain of politics. When such questions present themselves, in justice to my race, I make my position known and stand for what I see to be the right.

We cannot elevate and make useful a race of people unless there is held out to them the hope of reward for right living. Every revised constitution throughout the southern states has put a premium upon intelligence, ownership of property, thrift and character.

As an educator, and not as a politician, I strive in every honorable and rational way to encourage the wise and enduring progress of my people; for if all inspiration and hope of reward is to be denied them, they will be deprived of one of the greatest incentives to intelligence, industry, and righteousness. On the other hand, if they are encouraged in sensible and conservative directions they will grow year by year into contentedness and added usefulness.

—Booker T. Washington

In 1901, Washington became the first black person to visit the White House when Theodore Roosevelt invited him to dinner. This was met with extreme backlash from white people, especially in the South. But President Roosevelt continued to see Washington as a brilliant intellectual who specialized in racial matters, and he valued the unique perspective that Washington brought. This perspective was adopted by the next president as well, and William Howard Taft often sought Washington's counsel.

A Good Fight Fought

In 1915, while visiting New York City, Washington collapsed and was immediately taken into the care of a physician. He was given the news that his body was shutting down and he had only days to live. Ever longing for his beloved Tuskegee, he boarded a train and arrived in the early morning of November 14th. He died just a few hours later. He was only 59 years old.

Booker T. Washington's funeral was held at the Tuskegee Institute and attended by over 8,000 people. He is buried in the cemetery on campus—his gravesite standing as a memorial to a man born a slave who would inspire a generation to set aside bitterness and instead focus on creating value and prosperity for themselves through hard work and innovation. Washington refused to see himself and his people as a victimized class, standing, ever with hands outstretched, waiting for white politicians to repair centuries of wrongs.

Although he chose a different approach than Dubois, Washington worked to educate and empower blacks through education, entrepreneurship, property ownership, and accumulation of wealth, while laying the foundation for the civil rights movement by creating a generation of Americans who knew their value and could stand on their own—Americans who could take their fight for equality to the highest levels of government and *win*.

Robert
SMALLS

Smalls escaped slavery by commandeering a Confederate ship and sailing to freedom with his family and several others aboard. His tenacity later led Abraham Lincoln to accept African-American soldiers into the Union Army.

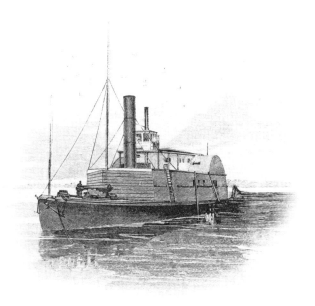

Slave, Pirate, Congressman

The city of Charleston, South Carolina lay sleeping during the hours before dawn on May 13, 1862. A soft, salty breeze brought with it the smell of the ocean and marshes. The only sounds to be heard were ships' bells and water splashing softly against the side of the Planter, a confederate steamer docked on the banks a mere handful of miles from Fort Sumter. You could almost hear the first shots of the American Civil War ringing through the air, though it had been over a year since they were fired.

Smoke curled in the air from the Planter, as Robert Smalls, a young slave who worked as part of the ship's crew, stood on the deck. The coming hours were crucial. He and his loved ones would either escape slavery or face certain death. This was the gamble that all runaway slaves took when seeking freedom. His future and that of his family would depend solely on his ability to maintain courage and calm as he executed the task at hand.

Like so many before and after him, Robert Smalls was terrorized by the thought that his young family—his wife and two children, both under five years old—might be separated and sold to new masters. He had heard whispers of coming changes and possible sales of slaves, and he knew, in that case, that the likelihood of their being separated was high. He would not allow it to happen.

Robert had no choice. He felt powerless and could think of only one way to be sure that his family could stay together forever: escape. These thoughts had planted themselves in his head years ago and now had grown into an idea that endlessly occupied his mind. Escaping on his own would have been hard enough, but with his young family it was seemingly impossible.

And the consequences of being caught… Robert couldn't bear to imagine what would happen to his beautiful wife and sweet children if he failed. So now, with a plan as terrifying as it was genius, he would put everything on the line to give his family and others a chance at a new, free life. Robert quietly notified the other enslaved crew members aboard the Planter that it was time to put their plan into action: they would seize the vessel and escape.

Robert's plan was to overpower the Confederate crew members, take over the Planter and deliver it to the fleet of Union vessels waiting just outside Charleston Harbor. The Union ships were strategically placed just outside Charleston in a naval blockade, in hopes of keeping imported goods from reaching the South. Charleston Harbor was a crucial port—it was one of the only ways to get goods to the Confederacy, since Fort Sumter had been taken. President Lincoln himself had ordered the blockade. He believed that if the Union could keep imported goods out of the south—goods like medicine, food, and cloth—the Confederacy would fall.

Robert and the other enslaved crew members managed to subdue the three officers on board the vessel without being spotted by the Confederate guards at the dock. Now that they had control of the ship, they needed to backtrack up the river without attracting the attention of other manned boats in the area, in order to rendezvous with Robert's wife and children and the families of the other slaves who were hiding in an abandoned ship moored to the shore. The only way Robert's plan could work was to make it seem as if all was normal—the Planter had to appear as if it were on an ordinary mission. The problem was that a Confederate ship captained by a black man would be seen as anything but ordinary. Also, the ship moving up the river would surely catch the attention of Confederate guards posted along the docks, and even if the waiting families somehow made it aboard, the large party would still have to sail through the heavily guarded harbor without being stopped or suspected.

Still under cover of darkness, Robert impersonated the captain by wearing a large straw hat similar to the one the captain usually wore. It wasn't much, but it was the only disguise he could find. Would it be enough?

A New Life

With the crew subdued and the straw hat pulled tight on his head, Robert captained the vessel away from port. The evening had been foggy, but now the sky was clearing, making the ship more visible. For a moment, Robert cursed his luck—he didn't want to be more visible to the Confederate guards keeping watch over the harbor. But as the fog lifted, he realized that the guards could now more easily see the Stars and Bars, and the Palmetto tree tucked under the crescent moon—the Confederate and South Carolina flags hoisted above the Planter. The guards noticed the Planter leaving and moved closer to see if anything was amiss, but all they saw was a Confederate ship and its Confederate crew.

They made their way downriver, preparing to rendezvous with Robert's wife and small children and the families of Robert's slave crew hidden on the abandoned boat. Smalls later recalled, "The boat moved so slowly up to her place we did not have to throw a plank or tie a rope," Luck was still on their side! The families slipped silently onto the

Planter, and they steamed along the river with the women and children hidden below deck. Smoke billowing, the mighty ship chugged along, leaving the Confederacy and slavery behind in its wake.

Now they faced the greatest danger. They were aboard a clearly marked Confederate steamer, and they were going to sail boldly into a Union blockade. Of course, the North would assume they were under attack and would prepare to fight.

Unless "Captain" Smalls and company could quickly convince the Unions ships that they were friendly, the Union soldiers would open fire—killing them all within seconds. Making it safely through seemed nearly impossible, but they had to succeed, not only to gain their own freedom, but to inspire others. Their story would breathe life, and hope, into the broken bodies and spirits of enslaved families all across the south. These thoughts calmed Robert's nerves and strengthened his resolve.

As the sun began to rise, ship and crew neared Fort Sumter. Every man, woman, and child on board was petrified—even Robert, but he took care not to let anyone see his fear. He knew they all depended on him, and he had to stay brave. One of the crew members on board would later recount, "When we drew near the fort every man but Robert Smalls felt his knees giving way and the women began crying and praying again."

In the early light of dawn, a Union ship came into view. The crew of the Planter rushed to lower the confederate flags and hoist a white flag of surrender. Their vessel was easily identified as a Confederate ship, so it was imperative that the Union soldiers see the white flag!

A thick fog began to seep into the air. Robert's heart sank. "Oh please, not now," he prayed. "Not after coming this far. Please let them see us. Please let them see the white flag."

All was still, and all was silent.

Suddenly, from the fog, a massive grey bulk came into view!

"Who goes there?" yelled the captain of the Union ship Onward.

"Good morning, sir!" came Robert's reply, "I've brought you some of the old United States guns, sir!—that were for Fort Sumter, sir!"

The Smalls family and company, were free at last.

No civilian, black or white, had ever provided such a large amount of supplies and weaponry to the Union cause. Robert's bravery and tactical prowess helped convince President Lincoln to allow black soldiers to serve in the Union army. Smalls served in the Union for the remainder of the Civil War and even captained the Planter as a Union vessel. He was a hero.

After the war, Robert became a politician. He founded the South Carolina Republican Party and served in the United States Congress.

A monument stands to commemorate the life of Robert Smalls in Beaufort, South Carolina. The inscription reads, "My race needs no special defense, for the past history of them in this country proves them to be the equal of any people anywhere. All they need is an equal chance in the battle of life."

Signers of the
DECLARATION

Committing an act of treason punishable by execution, these delegates signed their names to a letter declaring themselves, and the colonists they represented, free from Britain's rule.

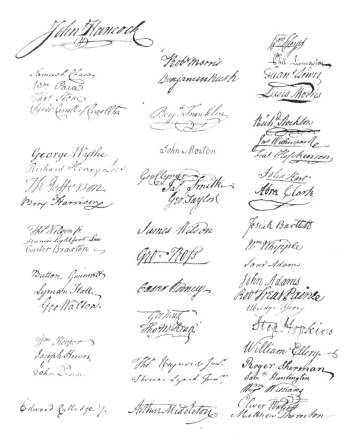

Toward Rebellion

The years leading up to the American Revolution were ones of distrust. Neighbor suspected neighbor as whispers of rebellion hissed through the streets. In musty basements and dimly lit corners of pubs, trusted allies spoke treasonous words, while those loyal to the crown watched for signs of mutiny.

Many men and women—citizens of Great Britain—found that they could no longer live under the conditions being pressed upon them by their king. They had hoped for a peaceful resolution to their complaints and had tried to make their concerns heard through official channels. They had resorted to protest and acts of rebellion when their pleas for justice went unheard. And still King George remained unsympathetic. Worse, he continued to raise their taxes and restrict the few liberties they still had.

Something had to be done.

A Declaration of Independence

When in the Course of human events it becomes necessary for one people to dissolve the political bands which have connected them with another and to assume among the powers of the earth, the separate and equal station to which the Laws of Nature and of Nature's God entitle them, a decent respect to the opinions of mankind requires that they should declare the causes which impel them to the separation.

Even the opening words of the Declaration hinted at the hope for a peaceful resolution. When Thomas Jefferson penned them, it's easy to picture him sitting at his desk, a myrtle wax and tallow candle burning late into the night as he deliberated over the phrasing he should use. How to tell the most powerful nation on earth that you were throwing off the legitimacy of its governance without inciting swift and terrible retribution?

Was it even possible?

As it happened, all the niceties Jefferson could muster couldn't have stopped the inevitable. The list of grievances presented to King George were too great to reconcile through peaceful channels. The die had been cast, as the last signer added his name and the ink spread into the parchment.

This meant war.

Lives, Fortunes, and Honor

When word reached England that the colonies had declared independence, the king signed an order condemning all fifty-six signers to death and branded them guilty of high treason. Great Britain reserved their most gruesome and severe punishments for those guilty of this charge. The punishment amounted to torture until death and then the desecration and scattering of the accused's body—denying them even a resting place or a gravesite for their loved ones to visit. The king supposed that the fear of such punishment would discourage others from supporting the dissenter's cause, but he was wrong.

Some imagine the founders of the United States as a group of wild and rebellious hotheads, young men with nothing to lose and an appetite for danger. What man, after all, with any sense of self-preservation, would pick a fight with the mightiest army in the world? But viewing them as young and reckless does these men a great disservice. The fact is, they had much to lose.

They had families—mothers, fathers, sisters and brothers, even wives and small children. Some of them owned fleets of ships; others, large and sprawling properties with homes full of valuable pieces of art and staffed with the best cooks and housekeepers that could be found in all the colonies. Most were respected businessmen, college graduates with loved ones both supportive of the patriot cause and loyal to their motherland. All were reluctant patriots who had plans for their lives and hopes for their futures—they weren't men who went looking for trouble.

But their government had become predatory—preying on the people instead of protecting them—and when governments begin to threaten the life, liberty, and property of the people they are supposed to protect, good men and women cannot sit by and do nothing. King George should have understood the commitment of the men who signed the Declaration when he read its closing line:

And for the support of this Declaration, with a firm reliance on the protection of Divine Providence, we mutually pledge to each other our Lives, our Fortunes, and our sacred Honor.

In signing the Declaration, these fifty-six men promised to commit the last of their resources and sacrifice everything they had—even their very lives—to the cause of securing the freedom of their fledgling nation.

Sacrifice in Action

The majority of men who signed the Declaration of Independence would survive the revolution. Many went on to have successful careers; two would even become presidents of the country they had helped liberate. But not all were blessed with such good fortune. Nine of the fifty-six signers would fall during the war, unable to ever relish the freedom they had given their lives to secure.

Less than a month after signing, Lewis Morris was targeted by British soldiers, who destroyed his home, stole his fortune, burned his land, slaughtered his cattle, and left him and his family running in fear for their lives.

Edward Rutledge, Arthur Middleton, and Thomas Heyward, Jr., suffered similar persecution when their homes and property were destroyed and their fortunes confiscated by the Crown. All three men would be captured in 1780 at the Battle of Charleston and would each spend a year in English prisons.

The world remembers Thomas Jeffereson's stylistic prose, John Adams' regal composure, the bespectacled Benjamin Franklin, and the cheeky John Hancock, who signed his name in a purposely large and flourished font so that "The fat old King can read it without his spectacles." We have named our memorials for them and commemorated them on our buildings, street signs, and even our currency.

But history has forgotten men like William Floyd, who was forced off the land that had been in his family for a hundred years when the British seized his home and turned it into a barracks for English troops. Does anyone remember

Hannah, William's sweet wife, who went into hiding with their three young children? They lived in exile for seven years, dependent on the mercy and support of others. Hannah died two years before the war ended, still living in exile and without a home of her own. She was buried in a small cemetery with a simple headstone that reads only, "Mrs. Hannah Floyd."

Thomas Nelson, Jr., who was born into a life of luxury, spent the Revolutionary War raising nearly two million dollars for the patriot cause and fighting with the militia. When British General Cornwallis seized Thomas' home during the battle of Yorktown, Thomas—ever the patriot—is said to have quietly given General Washington the "go ahead" to destroy it. Thomas would never regain his wealth. He died at the age of 50.

During the British assault on New York, Francis Lewis' home, property, and family were seized. His wife was taken prisoner and suffered such cruel treatment at the hands of her captors that she died within a year of her release, her body and spirit broken by the ordeal. Racked with guilt, Francis never remarried.

In every revolution, there are heroes, both sung and unsung, who sacrifice with no promise of victory or reward. They leave us stories of courage and bravery, and ask us to follow in their footsteps. They ask us to remember the lessons they learned and that wrong is wrong no matter who is doing it. They warn us that "A Prince, whose character is thus marked by every act which may define a Tyrant, is unfit to be the ruler of a free people."

William
WILBERFORCE

Showing the power of persistence, William fought against the slave trade for several decades as a member of Parliament before finally achieving victory, leading to the abolition of the slave trade in the British Empire.

AM I NOT A MAN AND A BROTHER?

Amazing Grace

The two Williams sat in front of the roaring fire in a room that would have been quite neat and stylish if not for the presence of a very large hare, two snoring dogs, six cats, sprawled and perched on various tables chairs and shelves, a wounded (but recovering) robin in a little box on the mantle, and a rather large garden snake coiled in the bottom of a vase on the side table. The visiting William kept cutting his eyes to the vase as his old friend spoke—suspicious of its occupant and doubtful of the sufficiency of weight possessed by the book that had been haphazardly placed on top. He felt that the owner of the home, the other William, didn't care nearly as much as he should about whether or not the snake remained in the vase.

As the fire roared and his friend spoke, his mind left the vase and its questionable occupant and wandered the path of the last twenty years.

Nary a Care

In 1776, William Pitt and William Wilberforce met at St. John's College. Pitt, the sober-minded son of the Prime Minister, was drawn to Wilberforce's jovial spirit and kind disposition. In many ways, the Williams were like night and day. Pitt was serious and studious, ever-mindful of his political ambitions and the large shoes he had to fill. Wilberforce, by contrast, seemed to hardly notice that he was at university at all, choosing instead to focus his time and considerable talent on entertaining all who happened upon him.

Known for his beautiful singing voice and witty retorts, William Wilberforce was the life of every party. It is said that the Prince of Wales once remarked that he would happily travel anywhere just to hear Wilberforce sing. He filled his days and nights with games of chance, lively debates, and too much food and drink. He bought horses and expensive clothes, but he was also generous and showed genuine concern for the needs and comfort of others. Although no one at Cambridge could have imagined it, William hadn't always been so light-minded and carefree.

An only child whose father died when he was very young, William had been sent to live with his aunt and uncle when he was only nine. He attended boarding school and spent summers and holidays in their care. During these formative years, he was introduced to evangelical Christianity, and he joyed in the freedom and excitement it offered in contrast to the dreary and stoic Church of England to which his mother and grandfather belonged. Religion became a source of happiness and excitement to him, and he relished every moment he was able to spend with his relatives. He especially adored his Aunt Hannah.

He often thought of God and of the poor and weak and afflicted. His mind wandered during his studies to songs he'd learned at church with Hannah and to the late night talks they had in front of the fire. To Hannah, and others like her, religion wasn't a box to check on Sunday—a somber hat one donned once a week and then set aside until it was needed again. Religion, to them, was who a person was—it was their every thought and word and deed. William loved thinking of his God and his religion in such joyful and human terms. He wrote home, excited to share his new faith and happiness with his mother, but his letters were not received in the spirit he'd hoped they would be. His mother and grandfather became gravely concerned for the well-being of young William. In these days, religious fervor was viewed as something tacky and unbecoming, reserved for the lower classes and those with mental deficiencies.

The decision was made to rescue William from this light-minded nonsense immediately, and so Williams' life changed again. He was snatched from the home and family he had come to know and love and brought back to live with his mother in Hull. Here, he was kept from the evangelical teachings which so inspired and uplifted him, and he fell into a period of reclusive sadness. He was twelve and had always been small for his age, prone to sickness, and troubled with weak eyesight that sometimes made reading difficult. He missed the way he felt with his Aunt and Uncle, and though his mother and grandfather tried to cheer him, none of their enticements could fill the emptiness he felt.

In time, William began to make friends. His years of religious excitement and the concern it filled him with for the poor and needy and oppressed began to fade into nothing but childhood memories. By the time he left for St. John's in the autumn of 1776, he had put away these childish things and had fully embraced all the distractions and enticements of high society. He attended balls, was a regular at the theater, and became quite fond of playing cards. This light-hearted entertainer is who William Pitt and others at Cambridge would know Wilberforce to be.

But the things that shape us in our youth often have a way of leaving lasting marks, and sometimes, the person we *really* are—even if we bury them or push them aside for many years—comes back to remind us that the world needs us to make more of ourselves.

William the Abolitionist

Somehow, Wilberforce managed to graduate from Cambridge, passing his exams without seeming to have ever opened a book or lifted a pen. Pushed on by Pitt, he decided to run for office, and by early 1780, both men had won their respective seats. They were only 21 years old.

Wilberforce quickly gained a reputation for his independent spirit in Parliament. Most members of Parliament, or MPs, were devoted to their party and voted strictly along party lines, but William refused to pick a side and chose instead to work with both political parties, depending on which position sat right with his conscience. His childhood sense of responsibility for those less fortunate and unable to advocate for themselves began to rise to the surface. William was becoming a moral force to be reckoned with.

Like-minded people seem to have a way of finding one another, and as word of William's passion for righting wrongs began to spread, a very special group of people found their way to him. They were an unlikely bunch: wealthy men and women, former slaves, eccentric preachers, and social outcasts—an odd lot, to be sure—but they were bonded in their common goal and believed that William Wilberforce was the key to their success. William had always found the practice of slavery abhorrent, but even he was not prepared for the things his new friends would show him.

One night, as he and his friends dined, a black man entered the room. William's friends introduced their host to Olaudah Equiano, a man born in Africa but captured by slave traders as a young boy. Equiano had been sent to the Caribbean, where he worked on sugarcane plantations until he was able to purchase his own freedom and escape to England a free man. He had written a book detailing the horrors of the Middle Passage—a route slavers took to transport their human cargo across the Atlantic Ocean. No one had ever shared a firsthand account of slavery the way Equiano did, and his story made William's blood run cold.

Where before, he had felt that slavery was immoral—an affront to God and to man—he now believed it to be the most evil institution the world had ever known. Equiano's stories of men, women, and children, crammed into ships, chained to each other in such cramped and filthy conditions that nearly a quarter of them would starve or die of illness on the eighty-day voyage, brought to William's knowledge a degree of human depravity and wickedness that he had never imagined.

Equiano's account consumed William. He thought of nothing but the plight of the poor Africans, snatched from their homes and forced to endure the most humiliating and degrading conditions one human being could inflict on another. He poured over Equiano's book, and he secured entrance to a slave ship and saw and smelled for himself the decks where proud and beautiful people were tortured and abused. If they somehow survived the journey, they would dock in the Caribbean, only to have their children torn from their arms, their families separated, and their lives purchased by the highest bidder. No relief awaited these men and women.

William's whole world became the plight of the African slave. He surrounded himself with fellow abolitionists, promoted Equiano's book, and arranged audiences for Equiano to share his accounts. He believed that if his countrymen knew the truth about the slave trade they would demand its abolition. And he was going to make sure they knew.

In 1789, William gave a speech before Parliament that would set in motion the work of the rest of his life:

When I consider the magnitude of the subject which I am to bring before the House—a subject, in which the interests, not of this country, nor of Europe alone, but of the whole world, and of posterity, are involved: and when I think, at the same time, on the weakness of the advocate who has undertaken this great cause—when these reflections press upon my mind, it is impossible for me not to feel both terrified and concerned at my own inadequacy to such a task. But when I reflect, however, on the encouragement which I have had, through the whole course of a long and laborious examination of this question, and how much candour I have experienced, and how conviction has increased within my own mind, in proportion as I have advanced in my labours;—when I reflect, especially, that however averse any gentleman may now be, yet we shall all be of one opinion in the end;—when I turn myself to these thoughts, I take courage—I determine to forget all my other fears, and I march forward with a firmer step in the full assurance that my cause will bear me out, and that I shall be able to justify upon the clearest principles, every resolution in my hand, the avowed end of which is, the total abolition of the slave trade. I wish exceedingly, in the outset, to guard both myself and the House from entering into the subject with any sort of passion. It is not their passions I shall appeal to—I ask only for their cool and impartial reason; and I wish not to take them by surprise, but to deliberate, point by point, upon every part of this question. I mean not to accuse any one, but to take the shame upon myself, in common, indeed, with the whole parliament of Great Britain, for having suffered this horrid trade to be carried on under their authority. We are all guilty—we ought all to plead guilty, and not to exculpate ourselves by throwing the blame on others; and I therefore deprecate every kind of reflection against the various descriptions of people who are more immediately involved in this wretched business.

Having now disposed of the first part of this subject, I must speak of the transit of the slaves in the West Indies. This I confess, in my own opinion, is the most wretched part of the whole subject. So much misery condensed in so little room, is more than the human imagination had ever before conceived. I will not accuse the Liverpool merchants: I will allow them, nay, I will believe them to be men of humanity; and I will therefore believe, if it were not for the enormous magnitude and extent of the evil which distracts their attention from individual cases, and makes them think generally, and therefore less feelingly on the subject, they would never have persisted in the trade. I verily believe therefore, if the wretchedness of any one of the many hundred Negroes stowed in each ship could be brought before their view, and remain within the sight of the African Merchant, that there is no one among them whose heart would bear it. Let any one imagine to himself 6 or 700 of these wretches chained two and two, surrounded with every object that is nauseous and disgusting, diseased, and struggling under every kind of wretchedness! How can we bear to think of such a scene as this? One would think it had been determined to heap upon them all the varieties of bodily pain, for the purpose of blunting the feelings of the mind; and yet, in this very point (to show the power of human prejudice) the situation of the slaves has been described by Mr. Norris, one of the Liverpool delegates, in a manner which, I am sure will convince the House how interest can draw a film across the eyes, so thick, that total blindness could do no more; and how it is our duty therefore to trust not to the reasonings of interested men, or to their way of colouring a transaction. "Their apartments," says Mr. Norris, "are fitted up as much for their advantage as circumstances will admit. The right ancle of one, indeed is connected with the left ancle of another by a small iron fetter, and if they are turbulent, by another on their wrists. They have several meals a day; some of their own country provisions, with the best sauces of African cookery; and by way of variety, another meal of pulse, &c. according to European taste. After breakfast they have water to wash themselves, while their apartments are perfumed with frankincense and lime-juice. Before dinner, they are amused after the manner of their country. The song and dance are promoted," and, as if the whole was really a scene of pleasure and dissipation it is added, that games of chance are furnished. "The men play and sing, while the women and girls make fanciful ornaments with beads, which they are plentifully supplied with." Such is the sort of strain in which the Liverpool delegates, and particularly Mr. Norris, gave evidence before the privy council. What will the House think when, by the concurring testimony of other witnesses, the true history is laid open. The slaves who are sometimes described as rejoicing at their captivity, are so wrung with misery at leaving their country, that it is the constant practice to set sail at night, lest they should be sensible of their departure. The pulse which Mr. Norris talks of are horse beans; and the scantiness, both of water and provision, was suggested by the very legislature of Jamaica in the report of their committee, to be a subject that called for the interference of parliament. Mr. Norris talks of frankincense and lime juice; when surgeons tell you the slaves are stowed so close, that there is not room to tread among them: and when you have it in evidence from sir George Yonge, that even in a ship which wanted 200 of her complement, the stench was intolerable. The song and the dance, says Mr. Norris, are promoted. It had been more fair, perhaps, if he had explained that word promoted. The truth is, that for the sake of exercise, these miserable wretches, loaded with chains, oppressed with disease and wretchedness, are forced to dance by the terror of the lash, and sometimes by the actual use of it. "I," says one of the other evidences, "was employed to dance the men, while another person danced the women." Such, then is the meaning of the word promoted; and it may be observed too, with respect to food, that an instrument is sometimes carried out, in order to force them to eat which is the same sort of proof how much they enjoy themselves in that instance also.

As to their singing, what shall we say when we are told that their songs are songs of lamentation upon their departure which, while they sing, are always in tears, insomuch that one captain (more humane as I should conceive him, therefore, than the rest) threatened one of the women with a flogging, because the mournfulness of her song was too painful for his feelings. In order, however, not to trust too much to any sort of description, I will call the attention of the House to one species of evidence which is absolutely infallible. Death, at least, is a sure ground of evidence, and the proportion of deaths will not only confirm, but if possible will even aggravate our suspicion of their misery in the transit. It will be found, upon an average of all the ships of which evidence has been given at the privy council, that exclusive of those who perish before they sail, not less than 12½ per cent. perish in the passage. Besides these, the Jamaica report tells you, that not less than 4½ per cent. die on shore before the day of sale, which is only a week or two from the time of landing. One third more die in the seasoning, and this in a country exactly like their own, where they are healthy and happy as some of the evidences would pretend. The diseases, however, which they contract on shipboard, the astringent washes which are to hide their wounds, and the mischievous tricks used to make them up for sale, are, as the Jamaica report says, (a most precious and valuable report, which I shall often have to advert to) one principle cause of this mortality. Upon the whole, however, here is a mortality of about 50 per cent. and this among negroes who are not bought unless (as the phrase is with cattle) they are sound in wind and limb. How then can the House refuse its belief to the multiplied testimonies before the privy council, of the savage treatment of the negroes in the middle passage? Nay, indeed, what need is there of any evidence? The number of deaths speaks for itself, and makes all such enquiry superfluous. As soon as ever I had arrived thus far in my investigation of the slave trade, I confess to you sir, so enormous so dreadful, so irremediable did its wickedness appear that my own mind was completely made up for the abolition. A trade founded in iniquity, and carried on as this was, must be abolished, let the policy be what it might,—let the consequences be what they would, I from this time determined that I would never rest till I had effected its abolition.

Although his speech failed to elicit enough support for the passage of his anti-slavery bill, its message spread through the country like wildfire—the abolitionist movement had sprung to life.

Among his newfound supporters was a young woman named Barbara Spooner. William had never given much thought to marriage, but in Barbara he found a place to rest. She brought clarity and calm to his troubled mind with her clear observations and knack for untangling the ever-racing thoughts vying for a place at the forefront of William's mind. She was beautiful, smart, witty, and talented. The two had a whirlwind romance, and eight days after meeting, despite concerned friends' pleas that they perhaps take things just a little bit slower, Barbara and William were married.

Try, Try Again

At the memory of Barbara and William's wedding day, Pitt's mind returned to his old friend's parlor. Remembering the snake, he cast a worried glance toward the side table and the vase. It was still securely capped with the suspect book, and as he breathed a small sigh of relief he returned his focus to his old friend's familiar voice. He smiled to himself at the realization that Wilberforce hadn't even noticed that Pitt hadn't been paying attention. He was talking about the bill he was about to bring before Parliament. This time, he was sure, it would pass.

Pitt admired his friend's passion. How many bills was this? Twelve? Thirteen? Twenty? He'd lost count. William Wilberforce had been introducing bills to end the slave trade ever since Pitt had been elected Prime Minister—he'd managed to fill his father's big shoes, afterall. William Pitt the Younger, they called him. It always made him laugh.

He was sick now. It seemed that he'd always been sick; his health had troubled him since he was a young man. But now something had changed. He knew he probably wouldn't see the end of the year.

He looked around the room again. It spoke of life and love. Every nook and cranny evidenced the spirit of the Wilberforce family. Books and animals crowded every surface. William had always loved animals and had a habit of domesticating things that, in the opinion of most, didn't belong in a person's home. At this thought, he checked the vase again. Pitt had been certain that marriage would tame William's eccentric nature, but instead of demanding that William abandon his unconventional hobbies and habits,

Barbara had simply joined him in them. They'd had five children together who were just as lovely and full of tenderness and compassion as their parents.

In quiet moments, Pitt had often contrasted his own life with that of his friend, William Wilberforce, the entertainer and wordsmith. The performer-turned-statesman-turned-abolitionist, husband, and father. What a full life he had lived, and how many lives he had touched! By contrast, Pitt's own life seemed rather insignificant. It was true that he had been the youngest man ever elected Prime Minister. He had led the nation through upheavals that had threatened to destroy the government and the monarchy. He had plenty to be proud of. But somehow he had forgotten to marry, always assuming that there would be time for that later. He hadn't fathered any children, and his home was always quiet and neat, everything exactly where he had left it, nothing out of place. They'd always been like night and day.

Oh, how he would miss his friend when he passed from this life. He hoped William's bill would succeed this time. Had there ever lived a man more worthy of success? Pitt could think of none.

Victory and Loss

William Pitt the Younger died at his home in the early hours of January 23rd, 1806. His death saddened his good friend, but it also reinvigorated him in his determination to win his cause. One year after Pitt's death, Wilberforce would bring his bill to abolish the slave trade before Parliament once more.

The deliberations lasted all night, but as he stood, making his final impassioned plea, he felt a shift in the air. A good speaker knows when he has hit on something that is being received well by his audience, and William felt it now. As he looked around at the faces of his fellow Englishmen, they didn't look away like they had in the past. They met his gaze—and held it. As his eyes swept the crowd, he saw heads nodding in agreement. Some men, with heads bent low, dabbed at the corners of their eyes or discreetly wiped their noses. The mood was somber, the air heavy and still with emotion.

The votes were read as the morning dawned. Men would later recall the golden rays of morning bursting into the chamber as Wilberforce stood, tears streaming down his face. The chamber erupted in applause as men who had for years stood in the way of William now stood to offer him praise.

When the vote was tallied, William's bill to abolish the slave trade throughout the empire of Great Britain was approved: 283 votes in favor and only 16 dissenting.

No longer would proud Africans be snatched from their homes and forced into the bellies of English ships. The Slave Trade Act received royal assent on 25 March 1807, and the world became a slightly better place.

30 More Years

The Slave Trade Act ended the trade of slaves throughout the British Empire, but it did nothing for those who were already enslaved. William knew that this must be his next fight—and fight he did.

He would introduce bills for the abolition of the practice of slavery for the rest of his life, and although his ill health caused him to give up public office in 1826, he never stopped advocating for the emancipation of all slaves. He gave his last speech as a guest before Parliament in April of 1833—nearly thirty years after the passage of the Slave Trade Act—and on July 26th, a messenger ran to the Wilberforce home to share the news with the bedridden abolitionist that his pleas had not fallen on deaf ears this time.

The English government had agreed to end the practice of slavery entirely.

The next day, William's frail condition worsened, and when Barbara rose early on July 29th, she found her beloved husband gone. He had passed sometime in the night, his spirit finally at peace with the knowledge that he had accomplished his life's work.

Sophie and Hans
SCHOLL

During the height of the Nazi regime's reign, when many people were compliant and quiet, the Scholl siblings, as part of the White Rose Society, were anything but.

EIN DEUTSCHES FLUGBLATT

DIES ist der Text eines deutschen Flugblatts, von dem ein Exemplar nach England gelangt ist. Studenten der Universität München haben es im Februar dieses Jahres verfasst und in der Universität verteilt. Sechs von ihnen sind dafür hingerichtet worden, andere wurden eingesperrt, andere strafweise an die Front geschickt. Seither werden auch an allen anderen deutschen Universitäten die Studenten „ausgesiebt". Das Flugblatt drückt also offenbar die Gesinnungen eines beträchtlichen Teils der deutschen Studenten aus.

Aber es sind nicht nur die Studenten. In allen Schichten gibt es Deutsche, die Deutschlands wirkliche Lage erkannt haben ; Goebbels schimpft sie „die Objektiven". Ob Deutschland noch selber sein Schicksal wenden kann, hängt davon ab, dass diese Menschen sich zusammenfinden und handeln. Das weiss Goebbels, und deswegen beteuert er krampfhaft, „dass diese Sorte Mensch zahlenmässig nicht ins Gewicht fällt". Sie sollen nicht wissen, wie viele sie sind.

Wir werden den Krieg sowieso gewinnen. Aber wir sehen nicht ein, warum die Vernünftigen und Anständigen in Deutschland nicht zu Worte kommen sollen. Deswegen werfen die Flieger der RAF zugleich mit ihren Bomben jetzt dieses Flugblatt, für das sechs junge Deutsche gestorben sind, und das die Gestapo natürlich sofort konfisziert hat, in Millionen von Exemplaren über Deutschland ab.

Manifest der Münchner Studenten

Erschüttert steht unser Volk vor dem Untergang der ...

White Roses in the Darkness

On a cold winter night in 1943, Hans Scholl, Alexander Schmorell, and Willi Graf were on their way to their local city center in Munich, Germany. The three young men belonged to a group called the White Rose—a group they had formed in nonviolent resistance against the Nazi regime. Although they were barely out of their teens, they were doing important (and dangerous) work. As was their habit, they were carrying hundreds of pamphlets detailing crimes committed by Adolf Hitler and his followers, the Nazis. Every chance they had, the young men unloaded their leaflets into mailboxes and slipped them into the coat pockets of passers-by. They believed the hearts of their fellow Germans would be softened if they were made aware of the terrible things their government was doing.

Hans, Willi, and Alexander were medical students attending the University of Munich, but years earlier, the three had served in the military, where they were stationed in France in the fight against Russia. While there, they witnessed what they viewed as atrocities committed by their own government against Jews and vowed that they would do all they could to put a stop to it.

Upon completion of their mandatory military service, they returned to their homes and families in Munich, where they joined with some of their classmates, including Hans's little sister, Sophie, in an effort to educate the people of Germany about what they had seen. With their youthful spirit, their religious convictions, and their impressive knowledge of German literature, the students began publishing their beliefs in pamphlets under the name White

Rose. The leaflets would later be known as "Leaflets of the Resistance."

On this particular cold winter night, the three friends had a daring and dangerous plan. In fact, it was so daring and so dangerous that Sophie could not sleep for worry about Hans and his friends. Her heart didn't stop racing until he finally returned home near dawn. Back at the university, Hans, Alexander, and Willi had pulled large tin stencils and white paint from their pockets and set to work. When students and staff arrived on campus the next morning, they were greeted with graffiti on walls and sidewalks.

DOWN WITH HITLER!

MASS MURDERER HITLER!

FREEDOM!

No one dared to even whisper words like these, and here someone had painted them boldly for all to see!

"We fight with our words," Sophie once said, and the words of the White Rose were beginning to catch the attention of the German people. Their words were also beginning to come to the attention of very dangerous people. Every member of the White Rose knew exactly what they were risking and understood the consequences if they were arrested for treason. Those who were caught and tried in the infamous Nazi "People's Court" were nearly always found guilty, and the penalty was almost always death. One member of the White Rose is quoted saying, "We were all risking our necks," and it was true.

After the first set of leaflets had been distributed, a second pamphlet was written and delivered in the dark of night, this one focused on the deportation and mass murder of Jewish citizens. They called it "a crime unparalleled in all of history." Soon, third and fourth leaflets were published, landing all over Munich and even in surrounding towns. They were stuffed into mailboxes, phone booths, and even public restrooms—the White Rose was everywhere.

"Hitler cannot win the war—he can only prolong it," the pamphlets promised, urging German citizens to rise up and reject their wicked government and the atrocities it was committing.

Every leaflet printed and distributed made the White Rose's discovery more likely. The Gestapo—the secret German police force meant to keep German citizens from rebelling against their government—scrambled to investigate the origin and location of the White Rose. They began looking for members, planting citizen-spies all over Munich with the promise of reward if members were found and arrested.

Sophie said, "What we wrote and said is also believed by many others. They just don't dare express themselves as we did." Her brother Hans agreed, saying, "It's high time that Christians made up their minds to do something… What are we going to show in the way of resistance… when all this terror is over? We will be standing empty-handed. We will have no answer when we are asked: What did you do about it?"

In the early morning of February 18, 1943, the sun was shining bright on the shoulders of Hans and Sophie Scholl as they made their daily walk to their university. Hans carried a small suitcase, and Sophie a briefcase. Inside, the siblings carried over two thousand copies of their latest leaflet. The campus was still; all the students were already in their classes. With their hearts threatening to beat out of their chests and the sound of their shoes clicking on the marble floor ringing in their ears, Hans and Sophie scattered leaflets down corridors and stacked them on bannisters. Planning to leave before classes let out, they entered the atrium of the Munich University main building and headed for the doors.

Looking into her briefcase, Sophie noticed a small bundle of leaflets she had missed. She grabbed them and quickly ran up the stairs and, just before the lecture hall doors opened, let them fly. She watched as they fluttered down in the early morning light and landed silently on the cold marble below.

But someone else had watched their silent flight. A custodian named Jakob Schmid turned quickly and walked into an office. Within minutes, Sophie and Hans were in Gestapo custody.

Perhaps predicting her fate, Sophie had once written, "How can we expect righteousness to prevail, when there is hardly anyone willing to give himself up individually for a righteous cause?"

Four seemingly endless days and nights of interrogation followed the Scholls' arrest. Initially, Hans and Sophie denied the accusations, but the evidence against them was too strong. When they realized there was no way out, they turned from trying to protect themselves to thinking only of protecting their friends. They took full responsibility for the White Rose and refused to name any co-conspirators.

Unfortunately, when Hans was arrested, he had a paper in his pocket that had incriminating details involving his friend and fellow member of the resistance, Christoph Probst, who soon joined the Scholls in prison.

On the 22nd of February, Hans, Sophie, and Christoph were brought into the German People's Court. As the three students and friends stood awaiting the verdict, they could hardly breathe. Hans and Sophie gripped each other's hands hard enough to nearly cut off circulation, and with heads held high, they prepared for the worst. The verdict was read, and it took them just a moment to register what they were hearing.

Schuldig.

Guilty.

Directly following their convictions, the siblings were taken to Stadelheim Prison to await their executions. As an act of mercy and in conflict with the rules of the prison, the siblings were allowed a short visit with their parents one last time. They sobbed and held each other close, while their father imparted his final words of wisdom to his children. "I'm proud of both of you," he said with a gentle smile, taking each of their faces in his hands and looking into their eyes. What brave and beautiful children he had been blessed with.

The other prisoners, and even the guards, were moved by the courage, love, and faith in God the two siblings showed in the face of such terrible circumstances. One guard later recalled, "They bore themselves with marvelous bravery." In their final moments together, the siblings are remembered to have said, "What we did will make waves."

At five in the evening on February 22, 1943, Sophie Scholl was brought to the execution chamber. Her last words were, "God, you are my refuge into eternity."

Moments later, Hans followed, and with his last breath, he cried out his final message of resistance: "Long live freedom!"

After the deaths of Hans, Sophie, and Christoph, despite being more aware than ever of the risk they were taking, the remaining members of the White Rose released another pamphlet. Their words reached farther than ever and were more widely read than any of the publishings that came before it. In bold lettering, it was titled: *Their Spirit Lives On!*

Dietrich
BONHOEFFER

While most of his fellow pastors were silent
or supportive of the Nazi regime's evils,
Dietrich's understanding of his Christian faith
compelled him to speak out and dissent.

A Family Heritage

On February 4th, 1906, in the town of Breslau, Germany, a set of twins were born—the sixth and seventh children in what would be a family of ten. The girl was named Sabine, and the boy Dietrich.

The Bonhoeffers were a wealthy family. Father Karl was a well-known psychiatrist and neurologist, and Paula, his wife, was a teacher. Paula and Karl came from long lines of artists, theologians, and great thinkers, and their children followed in the footsteps of their ancestors. Most of the Bonhoeffers set out boldly into the world, finding success and notoriety from a young age, and Dietrich was no exception.

Dietrich was a talented musician, and his family hoped he would make a name for himself as a pianist—he certainly had the ability—but he set his sights on theology and hoped to become an ordained minister. By the age of 21, he had earned his bachelor's and master's degrees from the University of Tübingen and his Doctor of Theology degree from Berlin University, but because he was still too young to be ordained, he traveled to the United States to teach and study there.

He was interested to learn how other countries taught and lived their faith, and although he was disappointed with the seminaries in the United States, he fostered meaningful friendships and saw firsthand the effect that racial segregation had on Christians. He began to see how churches could become politicized and how the doctrines of man could corrupt the doctrine of Christ.

His time spent in black churches across the United States and the lessons he learned about racial discrimination and its effect on the gospel would have a lasting impact on his life, shaping the work he would be drawn to upon his return to Germany in the early 1930s.

The Rise of a Wicked Man

In 1931, at the age of 25, Dietrich was ordained a minister. He immediately began teaching and made a name for himself as a promoter of inter-faith unity and adherence to the gospel of Jesus Christ as it was prescribed in the Bible. He felt that the modern church had become too worldly and had complicated what he saw as the simple doctrine of Christ. His sermons asked people to turn back to the plain and simple truths of the scriptures and the plea of Christ that his followers model their behavior after his perfect example. His messages were well received—people found comfort and truth in his ideas—but the political shifts taking place in Germany were about to send Dietrich on a new path, and his simple message would soon become controversial and even dangerous.

In November, 1932, the rising Nazi party staged what amounted to a poitical coup in churches across Germany. They ousted church leadership that wasn't overtly supportive of the Nazi party and replaced them with those who were. Dietrich saw danger and immediately spoke out, raising his voice to warn Christians in Germany that this path would lead to despotism and was not of God.

Adolf Hitler and his Nazis assumed power on 1 January 1933, and two days later, Bonhoeffer took to the radio to denounce the dictator and his party. He warned against idol worship, something he recognized in the German people who were totally swept up in admiration and adoration of their *Führer*. He warned what would happen should the people put their trust and faith in man instead of in their God, but his radio broadcast was cut off when he was mid-sentence. This was the first of many efforts the new German government would make to silence Dietrich Bonhoeffer.

Four months later, he delivered another radio address, this time specifically directing his message to Christians. He laid out in no uncertain terms the fact that the Nazis, under the direction of Adolf Hitler, were persecuting and brutalizing Jews and called on churches to organize and condemn the Nazis and Hitler. Instead, in August of 1933, the national church of Germany adopted what was called the "Aryan Paragraph" into their creed, effectively removing those with Jewish ancestry from any leadership position. A couple of months later, 20,000 German Christians rallied to petition the church to remove the Old Testament from the Bible.

Bonhoeffer's fears that National Socialism was corrupting the church and its followers were realized.

Facing the Music

The national church recognized Bonhoeffer's strength and ability to organize and move his followers, and they wanted to keep him within their fold, rather than have to deal with him as a potential enemy, so in the autumn of 1933, Dietrich was offered a ministerial position in Berlin.

He refused, telling church leadership that he would not be party to their pro-Nazi agenda and, instead, leaving the country to take a two-year assignment as a pastor in England. His friend, the famous Swiss theologian, Karl Barth, wrote to Bonhoeffer, taking him to task for leaving the country. He felt that Dietrich was taking the easy way out and that the church in Germany needed his leadership more than the church in England. Barth told him, "You are a German, the house of your church is on fire! You must return to your post by the next ship!"

The letter sat heavy on Dietrich's heart, and although he took the position in England, his friend's words weighed on his mind. While in England, he spread his message of a Christ-centered religion and tried to garner support for the anti-Nazi cause. The English government failed to respond to or acknowledge the warnings Bonhoeffer and others were giving about the true intent of Hitler and his Nazis, and in 1935, with Barth's words still ringing in his ears, he returned to Germany.

Bonhoeffer and his friends had started what was called the Confessing Church, which taught principles of Christ-centered living and accountability to God for what one contributes to the world and to those in it. Upon his return, he set about establishing seminaries across Germany, where ministers in this new faith would be taught the doctrine of the Confessing Church, but by the fall of 1937, the Nazis had made the preaching of their doctrine illegal, and Bonhoeffer and others were forced to go underground, teaching and worshiping in secret.

In 1938, Dietrich learned from his brother-in-law of a plot to assassinate Adolf Hitler by some people within the

German government. He also learned that war was coming and found himself in a difficult and frightening position. He had opposed war as a pacifist all his life, and he knew that staying in Germany would mean being conscripted, or drafted, into the war—something that he knew he couldn't in good conscience lend his service or support to. Uncertain of the best course of action, he took a teaching position in the United States and left Germany, his church, and Adolf Hitler behind.

Almost immediately after arriving in the United States, he realized he had made a mistake. He felt like a coward—how could he have left his countrymen and his church at this most dangerous time in an effort only to save himself from discomfort? Did he not believe that part of being a Christian was suffering discomfort and ministering amongst the sick and afflicted, even those who wished harm to Christ's followers? Was this theme not central to the doctrine that he preached? He wrote,

> I have come to the conclusion that I made a mistake in coming to America. I must live through this difficult period in our national history with the people of Germany. I will have no right to participate in the reconstruction of Christian life in Germany after the war if I do not share the trials of this time with my people ... Christians in Germany will have to face the terrible alternative of either willing the defeat of their nation in order that Christian civilization may survive or willing the victory of their nation and thereby destroying civilization. I know which of these alternatives I must choose but I cannot make that choice from security.

Convicted in the belief that he must face the troubles and dangers of his home country along with all the other Germans, he returned and, at his brother-in-law's recommendation, was accepted into the *Abwehr*—the German secret intelligence service. By joining the *Abwehr*, Dietrich was able to avoid conscription into the army and any chance of being forced to fight in the war. Although he still opposed the Nazi cause, he was able to position himself in a place that met his requirement to serve but still allowed him to live his non-violent lifestyle.

It also allowed him to see and hear the innermost workings of the Nazi regime.

Dietrich the Spy

From 1941 until 1943, Dietrich worked as a Nazi intelligence agent. It was during this time that he learned the full extent of the atrocities being committed by the Nazis against Jews and other minorities within Germany and the surrounding countries. Remaining close to those within the German Resistance Movement whom he had befriended through his anti-Nazi activism in earlier years, he began funnelling classified Nazi plans and information to the Resistance, using the inside information he had access to through his job to frustrate and sabotage the efforts of Hitler and his regime. He also used his position to help countless Jews arrange escape from Germany to Switzerland. He arranged a secret meeting with a member of the British House of Lords in the hopes, once again, that England would take the knowledge of the treatment of German Jews seriously and intervene, but once again his pleas were ignored. England did nothing.

On April 5, 1943, Dietrich Bonhoeffer was arrested and

taken to Tegel military prison. He remained jailed there for a year and a half, charged with being a spy and awaiting trial. He used his time in prison to write letters to the people he loved, and he taught his gospel of Christ-centered living and devotion to the truth of scripture to fellow prisoners. All who heard him preach were comforted and empowered by his messages. Even some of the prison guards were drawn to him, with one young man named Knobloch even offering to help him escape. Although the temptation was great, Dietrich feared Nazi retaliation against his family and friends if he escaped, so he made the difficult decision to remain imprisoned.

Trial and Punishment

On July 20, 1944, an assassination attempt was made on Adolf Hitler. A bomb was planted under a conference table next to Hitler by a young Nazi officer, but someone accidentally kicked it right before it was set to go off, and Hitler survived the blast. Enraged, he put all of his efforts into finding and arresting those responsible for the plot against him. Hitler's private police force, the Gestapo, made sweeping arrests across Germany in the following week, rounding up anyone who was even loosely connected to anyone who knew about the attempt on his life.

Dietrich's brother-in-law had been central to the planning of the assassination, and when word reached Hitler, Dietrich was transported from Tegel prison to Buchenwald concentration camp, and then on to Flossenburg concentration camp. Only a month later, on April 4th, 1945, the diaries of the head of *Abwehr* were discovered, revealing that the plot to kill Hitler had gone all the way to the top of the intelligence community. In a fit of rage, the *Führer* ordered the execution of everyone involved.

Dietrich was just wrapping up his Sunday sermon for his fellow prisoners when guards came to take him away. He turned to a young man in the ragged congregation and said, "This is the end—for me the beginning of life."

Three days later, he was tried before a makeshift court— denied any defense or opportunity to speak for himself and with no witnesses or record of court proceedings— and sentenced to death.

The next morning, stripped naked in an effort to humiliate the modest preacher, Dietrich was led to the gallows. Witnesses to the execution recalled that he conducted himself with grace and dignity, stopping for a moment to offer a humble prayer to his God.

In total, the Gestapo rounded up 7,000 Germans in connection with the 20 July plot to kill Hitler. Of the 7,000 arrested, 4,980 were executed. Most were tried in circus courts without any due process or defense, and those who weren't executed spent the remainder of the war in prisons and concentration camps.

Less than one month after the execution of Dietrich Bonhoeffer, Nazi Germany fell to the allied army, and prison camps across Germany and Nazi-held territory began to be liberated by U.S., Russian, and English troops. The atrocities committed by Adolf Hitler and his Nazis, which Bonhoeffer and many others had tried to bring to the attention of the world, were finally laid open for all to see.

A collection of the letters sent by Dietrich to his friends and family were compiled into a book called *Letters and Papers from Prison* and give a glimpse into the heart and mind of the gentle minister who chose life amongst the persecuted and oppressed—living, as Christ had, amongst his enemies and forsaking the comforts of an easy ministry.

Althea
GIBSON

Althea Gibson was an American tennis player and professional golfer, and one of the first black athletes to cross the color line of international tennis. In 1956, she became the first African-American to win a Grand Slam title and the Wimbleton cup.

Making a New Life

In 1927, a little girl named Althea was born to poor sharecroppers on a cotton farm in Clarendon County, South Carolina. Life was hard for her family, and by 1930, they had lost the farm and moved to Harlem, New York. Her parents, Daniel and Anna, had four more children after Althea, and life got harder still. There wasn't always enough food, and money was always tight for the Gibson family. Althea spent a lot of time walking the streets and getting in fights with other kids. Her father wasn't always a very nice man, and sometimes he hit Althea and her siblings. The more Althea got in fights in the neighborhood, the more she got hit at home, and sometimes she would live in a special home for kids whose parents didn't take good care of them.

Although her neighborhood was very poor, the community got together and blocked off part of the street every day so that the kids could play sports. The local police department even helped organize the games and keep the kids safe while they played. Althea found solace in the organized athletic events, and she soon began fighting less and playing sports more. She was particularly good at paddle tennis, a game kind of like tennis that was played on a hard court and with a solid racket.

By the time Althea was twelve, she was the New York City women's paddle tennis champion, but by the time she turned thirteen, she had returned to street fighting. Her father had taught her how to box, and she spent a lot of time practicing her skills on kids in the neighborhood that she had disagreements with. She dropped out of school and spent her time fighting, playing basketball, and watching movies. She didn't have a lot of interests and didn't have plans for her life, and often, when people don't have a lot of interests or a lot of plans for life, they don't have very bright futures.

But she still had paddle tennis, and one day, word reached someone from the Cosmopolitan Tennis Club that there was a talented little girl in Harlem who could beat anyone at paddle tennis. They went to watch her play and decided that with a little bit of training—and maybe some lessons in why it's not a good idea to punch people—she could be as good at tennis as she was at paddle tennis.

A New World

Althea was a natural!

She began to dominate the local tennis circuit almost as soon as she entered the sport, winning nearly every match she played. In 1942, the American Tennis Association, an organization that promoted and sponsored tournaments for black athletes, hosted a tournament nearby. Althea entered, and less than a year after picking up her first tennis racket, she won the tournament.

Althea's life changed after that. She continued to play in local tournaments and was noticed by a college scout for Florida A&M University. They offered her a tennis scholarship, and in a few years, the little girl from the failed cotton farm and the streets of Harlem was a college graduate and part of the United States Lawn Tennis Association, where she competed against some of the best tennis players in the country.

Althea's opportunities should have been unlimited, but it was 1950 in the United States, and the South's "Jim Crow" laws, which allowed white businesses to discriminate against black people because of their skin color, posed a real problem for her advancement in the sport.

Although the USLTA technically barred discrimination based on race, most of their tournaments were held at clubs that didn't allow black people. So Althea, one of the most talented and successful female tennis players the sport had ever seen, wasn't allowed to compete in the sport's biggest tournaments. Most people simply turned a blind eye to Althea's plight. Maybe they didn't mind judging people because of the color of their skin, or maybe they were afraid to compete against such a talented player, but whatever the reason, Althea was stuck in a position that wasn't her fault and that she couldn't do anything to fix.

Sometimes, when a person is being mistreated and isn't able to defend or advocate for themselves, a brave defender will step forward and speak on their behalf, and this is what happened for Althea. A woman named Alice Marble—a white woman who had won eighteen championships before retiring from tennis—wrote a letter that was published in the widely read magazine *American Lawn Tennis*, taking the organization to task for their unfair and unethical treatment of Althea Gibson and other players of color. She minced no words in voicing her disgust for the USLTA's treatment of Althea and described the loss that the nearly exclusively white sport would suffer if it ignored all of the talent of black competitors:

If tennis is a game for ladies and gentlemen, it's also

time we acted a little more like gentlepeople and less like sanctimonious hypocrites. If Althea Gibson represents a challenge to the present crop of women players, it's only fair that they should meet that challenge on the courts...

The entrance of negroes into national tennis is as inevitable as it has proven in baseball, in football, or in boxing; there is no denying so much talent. The committee at Forest Hills has the power to stifle the efforts of one Althea Gibson, who may or may not be succeeded by others of her race who have equal or superior ability. They will knock at the door as she has done. Eventually, the tennis world will rise up en masse to protest the injustices perpetrated by our policy makers. Eventually—why not now?

Alice's letter hit like a lightning bolt. Her opinion mattered, and her words had the desired effect. That year, Althea Gibson was invited to the Nationals. She made her debut on her 23rd birthday.

Within two years, Althea would be ranked 10th in the world, and by 1955, she was on a world tour competing against the best tennis talent on the planet. In 1956, she won the French Open, and in 1957, she won at Wimbledon. Her trophy was presented by Her Royal Highness Queen Elizabeth II. Althea would later call 1957 "The Year of Althea Gibson," saying, "Shaking hands with the queen of England was a long way from being forced to sit in the colored section of the bus." When she returned to the United States, she was honored with a ticker tape parade in New York City where she was awarded the Bronze Medallion—the city's highest civilian award—by the mayor. Just two months later, she would win the U.S. National Championship.

In 1957 and 1958, Althea was named Female Athlete of the Year and became the first black woman to appear on the cover of *Sports Illustrated* and *Time* magazines. She retired from tennis in 1958 and spent the rest of her life teaching and mentoring others. Althea Gibson had won 56 nation and international titles and broken every barrier placed in her path.

Katrina Adams, the first black president of the United States Tennis Association said, "This is not just a player who won a ton of titles—this is someone who transcended our sport and opened a pathway for people of color." She continued, "If there was no Althea, there'd be no me, because tennis would not have been so open to me. Everything she had to do was three times harder than it was for the normal person."

Although many who have followed her in footsteps have viewed her as a trailblazer and a hero, Althea remained humble. In her autobiography, she wrote, "I never regarded myself as a crusader, I don't consciously beat the drums for any cause, not even the negro in the United States. I don't want to be put on a pedestal. I just want to be reasonably successful and live a normal life with all the conveniences to make it so. I think I've already got the main thing I've always wanted, which is to be somebody, to have identity. I'm Althea Gibson, the tennis champion. I hope it makes me happy."

Althea could have lived her life on the streets, never meeting her potential and always making excuses for her failures. she certainly suffered enough hardships to justify quitting—or never starting to begin with. But that would have been the easy path, and Althea Gibson never did take the easy path.

Katherine
JOHNSON

As one of the first African-American women to work as a NASA scientist, Katherine Johnson had to navigate racial and gender barriers to help the first manned spaceflight missions succeed.

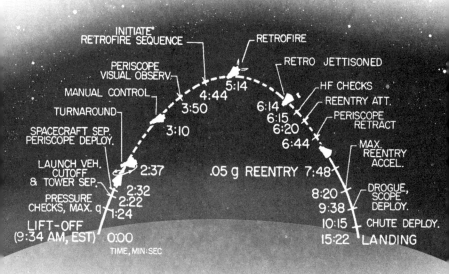

INITIATE
RETROFIRE SEQUENCE ——— ┌— RETROFIRE

PERISCOPE
VISUAL OBSERV.   ┌— RETRO JETTISONED

MANUAL CONTROL   5:14
                        4:44   ┌— HF CHECKS
TURNAROUND   3:50   6:14 ┌— REENTRY ATT.
                                6:15 ┌— PERISCOPE
SPACECRAFT SEP.   3:10   6:20   RETRACT
PERISCOPE DEPLOY.   6:44

LAUNCH VEH.   MAX.
CUTOFF   REENTRY
& TOWER SEP.   2:37   ACCEL.

PRESSURE   2:32   .05 g REENTRY 7:48   ┌— DROGUE,
CHECKS, MAX. q   2:22   8:20   SCOPE
                  1:24   9:38   DEPLOY.
LIFT-OFF   10:15 CHUTE DEPLOY.
(9:34 AM, EST) 0:00   15:22 LANDING
                TIME, MIN:SEC

A Path to Success

Katherine Johnson was hand-selected by the president of West Virginia University to be one of three black students—and the only woman—to start the integration process in the graduate program of the formerly whites-only school. This accomplishment alone was notable enough, yet it paled in comparison to what she would go on to achieve.

Katherine was born in 1918 in White Sulphur Springs, West Virginia. From a young age, she had a curiosity and thirst for knowledge that was unmatched by her peers and allowed her to skip several grades. She graduated from high school at the age of fourteen and had graduated college with degrees in mathematics and French by the time she turned eighteen. Katherine's mind was so remarkable and her ability to solve complex equations so uncommon that her college professors added entirely new courses just for her.

After graduating college, she took a job as a teacher and married a kind man named James Goble. James always supported Katherine in her work and encouraged her to enroll in the graduate program she'd been selected for. He knew that his wife had an uncommonly brilliant mind, and he wanted to see her accomplish as many things as she set her mind to.

But what Katherine wanted most was to be a wife and mother, so when she became pregnant only a year into grad school, she happily quit in order to focus on raising a family. She and James had three daughters, and family life was happy. Katherine worked as a teacher, which enabled her to spend a lot of time with her children; she had the best of both worlds!

Computers in Skirts!

At a family reunion in 1952, a family friend mentioned that the National Advisory Committee for Aeronautics was looking for mathematicians. James encouraged Katherine to apply, and in 1953, she was hired on by the Langley Memorial Aeronautical Laboratory where she worked in the Guidance and Navigation Department. Katherine quickly made a name for herself as a hard worker and a reliable mathematician—she was never wrong! She loved her work, and those she worked with loved her! The National Visionary Leadership Project recorded that,

> At first she [Johnson] worked in a pool of women performing math calculations. Katherine has referred to the women in the pool as virtual "computers who wore skirts." Their main job was to read the data from the black boxes of planes and carry out other precise mathematical tasks. Then one day, Katherine (and a colleague) were temporarily assigned to help the all-male flight research team. Katherine's knowledge of analytic geometry helped make quick allies of male bosses and colleagues to the extent that, "they forgot to return me to the pool." While the racial and gender barriers were always there, Katherine says she ignored them. Katherine was assertive, asking to be included in editorial meetings (where no women had gone before). She simply told people she had done the work and that she belonged.

Although Katherine worked in a white male-dominated industry, she would recall that she never felt like she was a victim of discrimination because she was black. She would remark that it was almost harder to be a woman in her field than it was to be black. Although women did much of the computing work that enabled the male engineers to do their jobs, they were always kept in the shadows and rarely given credit for their contributions.

But Katherine never was one to sit back and wait for someone to recognize her talent. She knew what she was capable of, and she always advocated for herself:

> We needed to be assertive as women in those days – assertive and aggressive – and the degree to which we had to be that way depended on where you were. I had to be. In the early days of NASA women were not allowed to put their names on the reports—no woman in my division had had her name on a report. I was working with Ted Skopinski and he wanted to leave and go to Houston ... but Henry Pearson, our supervisor—he was not a fan of women—kept pushing him to finish the report we were working on. Finally, Ted told him, "Katherine should finish the report, she's done most of the work anyway." So Ted left Pearson with no choice; I finished the report and my name went on it, and that was the first time a woman in our division had her name on something.

Katherine would continue to break barriers with nothing but her sharp mind and her determination to do her best and to see every project she began through to the end, no matter how complex or difficult.

Although Katherine was enjoying tremendous success in her career, her personal life was difficult. Her beloved husband had been diagnosed with an inoperable brain tumor, and she spent as much time as she could with him and their three young girls. In 1956, James succumbed to his illness, and Katherine found herself a widowed mother of three. Her most important job was still that of mother, and even though she spent her days calculating trajectories of rocket ships, her little family was always her biggest priority.

Somehow, with the help of family and friends, Katherine and her girls managed to shape a new life without James. They all missed him and loved him dearly, but they were determined to be happy in spite of the hardships they had suffered. There was always laughter and songs at bedtime in the Gobles' home, and in time, Katherine met another kind man who supported her in her endeavors. His name was Jim Johnson, and although they never had children together, he loved and raised Katherine's girls as his own.

To the Moon!

Katherine was an invaluable contributor to the United States space program. In 1961, she calculated the trajectory of astronaut Alan Shepard's famous flight, helping him become the first American in space! In the 1960s, NASA began using machines for computations instead of people, but they were leery of the new technology and needed to make sure that the complex calculations were right. So what did they do? They had Katherine Johnson check the computer to make sure it had figured the equations correctly. Imagine being so good at math that people asked you to check the work of a computer for accuracy!

As NASA was preparing to send the first man into orbit in 1962, Katherine was selected to do her most famous work. The mission of John Glenn was so complex, so intricately planned, that it was necessary to construct a worldwide communications network that linked tracking stations around the world to the IBM computers in Washington, Cape Canaveral, and Bermuda. The computers themselves were programmed with the equations that were responsible for calculating the trajectory of the shuttle for Glenn's Friendship 7 mission. However, those computers were subject to blackouts and technical errors, so while running through the pre-flight checklist, Glenn personally asked for Katherine Johnson to recheck the equations herself. Glenn and his crew had far more faith in Katherine than in the machines. He was quoted as saying, "If she says they're good, then I'm ready to go."

Thanks to all the hard work and countless hours of calculations and equations done by the crew and Johnson, Glenn's mission was a shining success and marked a turning point in the space race between the Soviet Union and the United States.

Some of Katherine's most impactful work came with the introduction of new technology to NASA and the space task force. She was integral in programming the computers so that they ran the equations with 100% accuracy every single time. Katherine's reputation for accuracy and honesty helped NASA integrate computers fully into the space program. She worked directly with the new digitized systems, and her involvement in their programming helped others at NASA accept the new technology. They trusted Katherine, and because she trusted the computers, they did too.

In 1970, Katherine and some of her colleagues gathered around a small black and white television and watched the grainy footage of Neil Armstrong taking the first steps on the moon. Katherine's equations had once again helped make history. She would continue to contribute to advancements in space travel and exploration, working on the Apollo 13 mission, as well as plans for possible missions to Mars later in her career.

Katherine retired from NASA in 1986, having worked for 33 years in the U.S. Space Program. She was awarded by presidents, honored by colleges and universities, immortalized in statues, written about in books, depicted in movies, and she even had a Barbie doll made in her likeness. She never stopped working to advance the cause of women in science and mathematics and encouraged all of her students, her six grandchildren, and her eleven great-grandchildren to pursue careers in science, technology, engineering, and mathematics (STEM).

She said, "We will always have STEM with us. Some things will drop out of the public eye and will go away, but there will always be science, engineering, and technology. And there will always, always be mathematics."

Katherine and Jim were married for sixty years. He died in 2019, and she followed him less than a year later. She was 101 years old.

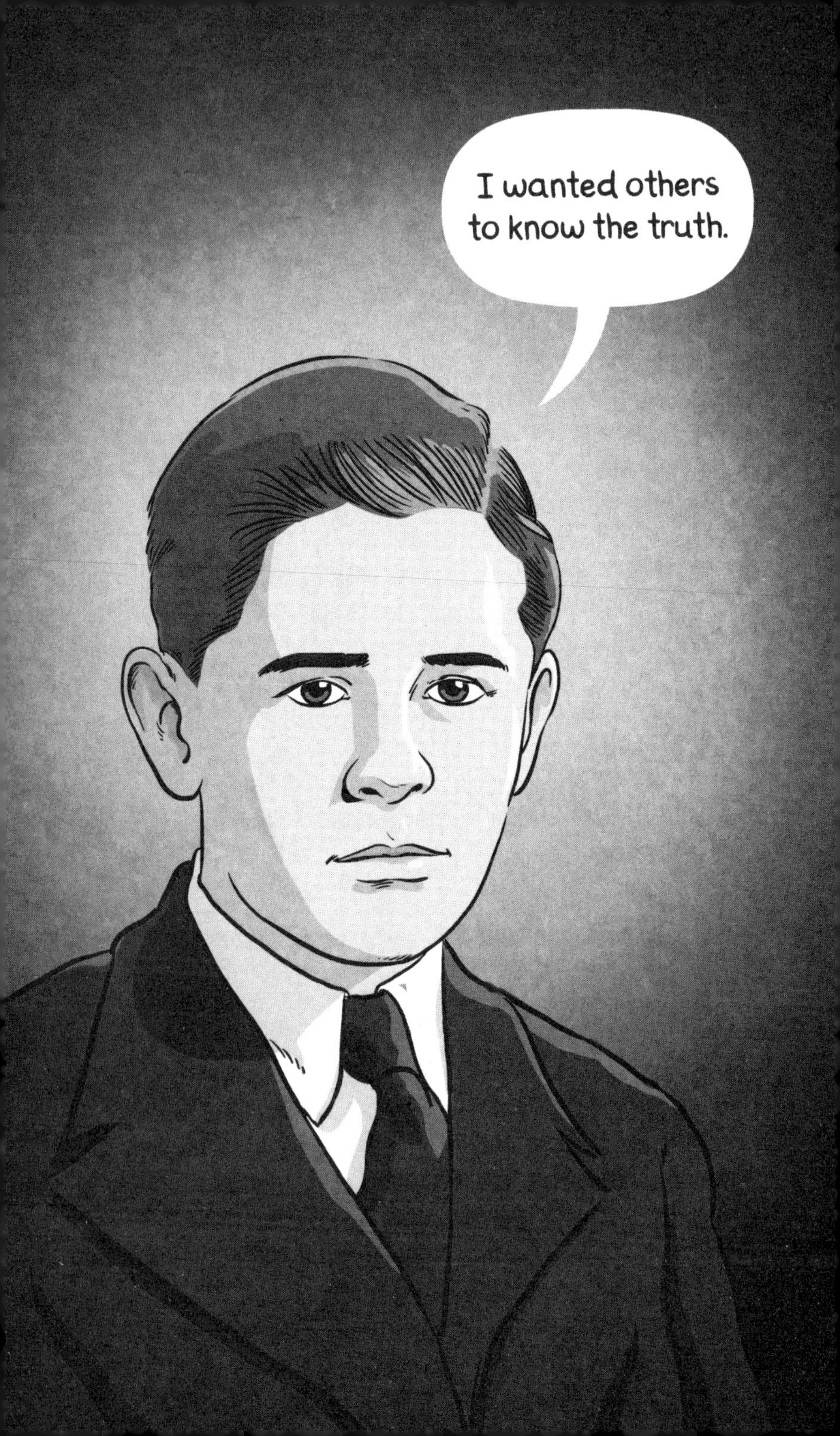
I wanted others to know the truth.

Helmuth
HÜBENER

Persuaded by his religious convictions and sense of justice, young Helmuth spoke out against the Nazi regime and tragically became the youngest person that the Third Reich sentenced to death and executed.

A Fight for Freedom

In the early morning cold of January 8, 1925, in the city of Hamburg, Germany, a little boy was born. His mother held him close to her chest, and looked into his bright blue eyes. She smiled, as all mothers do, and imagined all the good that her little son would bring to the world. He was called Helmuth, and—just as his mother had known he would—he grew into a kind and thoughtful child who loved his family and his friends and was active in his church and in the Boy Scouts.

When Helmuth was eight, a man named Adolf Hitler rose to power in Germany. When Helmuth was ten, Hitler made it illegal for the Boy Scouts to gather in Germany— he wanted all young men to join the Hitler Youth and all young girls to join the League of German Girls. Helmuth loved the Scouting program, and he was sad to see it go, but he joined the Hitler Youth along with the other boys his age.

When Helmuth was thirteen, something happened that changed his feelings about the Hitler Youth. One night, people all over Germany went out into the streets of Jewish towns and villages and began breaking windows and destroying property. Jewish churches—called synagogues— were burned down, and when frightened men, women, and children ran out of the burning and damaged buildings, they were hit and kicked and thrown to the ground.

Many of the Hitler Youth and their parents participated in this violent and bloody display of hatred and abuse, and when the sun rose on the morning of November 10, 1938, the streets were blanketed with shattered glass.

The Night of the Broken Glass

After *Kristallnacht*, or The Night of the Broken Glass, everything seemed different to Helmuth. He had always been a gentle and kind-spirited boy, and he couldn't understand why people would cause so much harm and treat others so cruelly. He believed that every person was his brother or sister. He had learned in church that everyone was a child of God, and he treated all he met with love and respect. Helmuth didn't like the things he was starting to see his leaders—and even some people in his church—say and do to Jewish people.

Most of Helmuth's church didn't agree with what the followers of Adolf Hitler—the Nazis—were doing, but there were just enough people in the Hubeners' small congregation speaking out in support of the Nazis that Helmuth found himself at odds with his fellow worshippers. That small group of Nazi supporters were able to convince the rest of the congregation that Jews shouldn't be allowed to come into their church buildings. Helmuth was thankful to have a close friend at church, a boy named Rudi Wobbi, who agreed with him, and the two boys often argued with other members of their church who sympathized with the Nazis.

The years passed, and the persecution of Jews by the citizens of Germany and the followers of Adolf Hitler continued to worsen. In 1941, at the age of sixteen, Helmuth started an apprenticeship at Hamburg Social Authority, where he made friends with a boy named Gerhard Düwer, who showed him how to listen to enemy broadcasts on a shortwave radio. Germany was at war, but the government wasn't honest with the German people about what was happening.

Adolf Hitler had a whole team of men and women whose only jobs were to distribute propaganda—misleading information—to the citizens of Germany. They broadcast fake news stories on the radio, and they wrote fake stories in the newspaper. They carefully crafted the stories that the German people heard, painting a picture of Germany winning battle after battle and fighting a moral and just cause. But what Helmuth and his friends heard on the Allied radio broadcasts told a very different story.

The boys came to see it as their duty to help the German people see through the lies and propaganda of the Nazis. They knew that listening to enemy radio stations and speaking out against Adolf Hitler were crimes. They'd heard stories of people who questioned the propaganda— or spoke out against Hitler—being taken in the middle of the night and, shipped off to camps, never to be heard from again.

They chose to speak out anyway.

A Dangerous Business

The boys began typing up leaflets on the church typewriter and writing the messages from the Allied broadcast on small pieces of paper. They carried them in their pockets and dropped them on street corners or slipped them into the pockets of people they passed on the street. They knew they had to be very careful not to let anyone see what they were doing. The leaflets carried messages about battles the German army had lost. They also carried tales of dark things Adolf Hitler and those closest to him were doing to people within Germany who tried to speak out against the Nazis.

One historian wrote, "Hübener's actions were extremely risky. Radio had helped the Nazis rise to power by spreading their messages to a mass audience. Once the Third Reich took over Germany, they began to use the radio to control the population. They flooded the airwaves with propaganda broadcasts, spreading false reports of glorious victories and bright prospects where there were none." In one of his leaflets, Hubener wrote:

> German boys! Do you know the country without freedom, the country of terror and tyranny? Yes, you know it well, but are afraid to talk about it. They have intimidated you to such an extent that you don't dare talk for fear of reprisals. Yes you are right; it is Germany – Hitler Germany! Through their unscrupulous terror tactics against young and old, men and women, they have succeeded in making you spineless puppets to do their bidding.

What Helmuth and his friends were doing had the potential to bring serious harm to the German cause. If they succeeded, they could affect the outcome of the war! But if they failed—if they got caught—they could be killed.

In February of 1942, Helmuth was hunched over a counter at Hamburg Social Authority. He was concentrating hard on trying to translate his pamphlets into French so that he could distribute them to prisoners of war, when he was noticed by a coworker named Heinrich Mohn. Mohn was a Nazi, and he immediately ran to get the police.

Helmuth was thrown in jail.

It was uncommon—even amongst the Nazis—to imprison someone as young as Helmuth, and his mother thought that despite the serious charge of treason, her son might be spared and turned over to her care. Helmuth's lawyer, his mother, and even some of the police who had arrested him, pled his case before the judge.

"Helmuth had always been an honest young man. He confessed to his crimes—he didn't lie—and that showed good moral character," they argued to the judge. "He was just a child—barely seventeen, and too young to understand the seriousness of the crimes with which he'd been charged," his mother said. "Surely, his arrest and imprisonment had taught him a lesson—this was a simple case of youthful rebellion and he had now gotten it out of his system," offered the arresting officer.

But all pleas for leniency fell on deaf ears.

The judge noted that Helmuth did indeed have an impressive character for one so young. It was true that he showed above-average intelligence for a boy of only seventeen, he agreed. In the judge's mind, these reasons made Helmuth even more dangerous to the Nazi cause. Someone so brave, so smart, and so strong could not be allowed to inspire others. He must be made an example.

And so, the order came: Seventeen-year-old Helmuth Hubener was guilty of treason. The sentence was death.

When Helmuth heard his fate, he stood up and shouted at the judge, "Now I must die, even though I have committed no crime. So now it's my turn, but your turn will come."

Later, his family would learn that he and his friends had made a pact. They promised each other that if they were arrested they would take all the responsibility for the writing and distributing of the leaflets on themselves. They would do everything they could to keep the attention of the Nazis away from the others. Even in the moment he learned he would be killed, Helmuth's concern was for others, as he tried to keep the judge's anger turned only toward himself.

The time he spent in prison between his sentencing and his execution was very hard. He suffered much mistreatment at the hands of his captors, who denied him every comfort and even his basic human dignity. Throughout his imprisonment, he remained faithful to his God and to his cause—he knew that he had done the right thing, and he was prepared to accept the consequences.

His sentence was carried out on October 27th, 1942.

Before his execution, Helmuth wrote a letter to his friend:

> I am very grateful to my Heavenly Father that my miserable life will come to an end tonight—I could not bear it any longer anyway. My Father in Heaven knows that I have done nothing wrong… I know that God lives and He will be the Just Judge in this matter.
>
> I look forward to seeing you in a better world!
>
> Your friend and brother in the Gospel,
>
> Helmuth

Helmuth Hubener stood up not only to his enemies but to friends, police, and even church leaders. He couldn't be convinced that something was right when he knew in his heart it was wrong. His story has taught all who hear it that doing what is right takes a lot of courage—and sometimes requires tremendous sacrifice. Helmuth gave his life to help others live free.

He was a hero.

Harriet Beecher
STOWE

A prolific writer and supporter of the Underground Railroad, Harriet authored *Uncle Tom's Cabin* to draw attention to the awful treatment of black slaves and help fan the flames in support of abolition.

A Book that Started a War

On a bright, summer day in 1811, in the tiny town of Litchfield, Connecticut, Roxana and Lyman Beecher welcomed their sixth child into the world. They called her Harriet, and as her mother cradled her gently, and her father brushed the baby-soft hair on her little head, their minds swirled with the hopes and dreams that fill the heads of all parents. They imagined all the things Harriet would do, all the people she would help, and all the lives she would surely touch.

Of course, the Beechers imagined their daughter would do good and important things. After all, this was the way the Beechers lived. Lyman was a beloved minister, and Roxana was a devoted mother and wife. Her faith was firmly rooted in her husband's preaching, and she raised her children to love God, love each other, and love their fellow man. The Beechers believed that all children—girls and boys—should receive a proper education, and Roxana devoted most of her hours to teaching and guiding her children, training them up to take their unique stations in life. Eventually, Lyman and Roxana would have eleven children, but their happiness would not be lasting.

When Harriet was just five years old, her sweet mother died, leaving Lyman to carry on alone and fill the place of nurturer, educator, and spiritual guide to his children. Recognizing his limitations in meeting such a mighty task, he enlisted the help of Harriet's older sister, Catherine.

Catherine ran a school, the Hartford Female Seminary, that offered something most schools didn't: a full, classical education for young ladies. Modeling her school after the way her mother raised her, Catherine believed that girls should be educated not just in housekeeping, needlepoint, and the finer, gentler areas of study traditionally taught to the fairer sex, but also in math, the sciences, and languages, subjects usually reserved for boys.

While at school, Harriet began to show promise as a writer. Her teachers marveled at her talent and encouraged her to dedicate time and effort to nurturing it. They knew what all wise teachers know—that children, when left to follow their interests and talents, often find their way into exactly the roles the world needs them to assume. Harriet was finding her way.

A Proper Author

In 1832, Harriet's father was offered a job presiding over the newly formed Lane Seminary in Cincinnati, Ohio. Harriet was 21 and felt that she had learned all that Litchfield had to teach her. She had spent the last several years teaching at her sister's school, and she was ready to move on to bigger and more challenging things. Several years earlier, Lyman had married a woman who shared the same name as Harriet, and so it was that Harriet, her step-mother Harriet, and the rest of the Beecher household set off on a grand adventure.

Harriet's world sprang wide open as she journeyed west. She had never seen such beautiful countryside, and she filled journals and sketchbooks with notes and observations of the unique wildlife and terrain. Before she had even settled into her new home, she had begun her first book. It would be published a year later, somewhat underwhelmingly titled,

Primary Geography for Children. But despite the boring title, Harriet was thrilled. She was an author!

When Harriet was twenty-five, she met a man named Calvin Stowe, who taught at Lane Seminary with her father. The two quickly fell in love and married within a year of meeting, with the blessing of Lyman and the rest of the Beecher family. Calvin was a kind and loving husband who encouraged Harriet to pursue her love for writing. The Stowes began their life together united in their faith, their mutual respect for one another, and their growing support for the abolitionist movement.

Slavery had been a part of life in the United States for as long as anyone could remember, but growing up in Connecticut and then moving to Ohio, Harriet had been sheltered from the knowledge of its most brutal practices. As the Stowes began to build their family—they would eventually have seven children, including a set of twins!—they witnessed riots and upheavals between anti-abolitionists and freed slaves in Cincinnati and along the Ohio River. Harriet and Calvin were appalled at the treatment of black women and men and vowed to help in any way they could.

Over the next several years, as Harriet continued to write for magazines and other small publications, the Stowe home became a stop on the Underground Railroad—a secret route slaves took when fleeing their masters in the southern states in the hopes of gaining their freedom in the North. By 1850, when Congress passed the Fugitive Slave Act, which made it a crime to help black men, women, and children escape slavery, the Stowes had moved to Maine. They now lived far enough north that they could no longer be of any help to slaves on their escape. But

Harriet remained troubled by the plight of those who were willing to risk their lives to escape being owned and traded as property—human beings who were commonly treated with less dignity and respect than common farm animals.

In late July 1849, Harriet and Lyman suffered a heartbreak that would change the course of history for their family and even, it could be said, for the whole United States.

Uncle Tom's Cabin

Sometimes, even though we care about someone else's plight, and even though we sympathize with them and want to help make their life easier, or safer, or better, we cannot truly know how they feel until we experience something that brings us closer to them through a trauma of our own.

On the morning of July 23rd, Harriet awoke to cries from the nursery. She rushed to the crib of her eighteen-month-old son, Charley, and found him gravely ill. A cholera outbreak had swept the city, and Harriet knew, as she looked at her sweet, sick little boy, that he had been infected. There was no cure for cholera at the time, and all Harriet could do was hold her son and try to make him comfortable as the disease racked his little body.

Death came quickly to cholera victims, and so it was for little Charley. Harriet recognized his swift passing as a tender mercy—an end to his suffering—but her heart was broken.

Two days after his death, she wrote a letter to her husband:

> July 26, Mr dear Husband, At last it is over and our dear little one is gone from us. He is now among the blessed. My Charley, my beautiful, loving, gladsome

baby, so loving, so sweet, so full of life and hope and strength, now lies shrouded, pale and cold, in the room below. Never was he anything to me but a comfort. He has been my pride and joy. Many a heartache has he cured for me. Many an anxious night have I held him to my bosom and felt the sorrow and loneliness pass out of me with the touch of his little warm hands. Yet I have just seen him in his death agony, looked on his imploring face when I could not help nor soothe nor do one thing, not one, to mitigate his cruel suffering, do nothing but pray in my anguish that he might die soon. I write as though there were no sorrow like my sorrow, yet there has been in this city, as in the land of Egypt, scarce a house without its dead. This heartbreak, this anguish, has been everywhere, and when it will end God alone knows.

As Harriet grappled with the grief of losing her young son, her heart was turned to the suffering of other mothers. She recalled tales she had heard: families standing on slave auction blocks, with some of the family being sold to this landowner and the rest to another; a husband shackled and carted off to Georgia, his wife struggling to hold onto her children as her new owner pushed and shoved her into a wagon bound for South Carolina; their children, some barely out of diapers, separated and dispersed to wealthy merchants and tobacco farmers on plantations across the South. The thought of this cruelty and injustice pressed down so heavily upon Harriet's small shoulders that she felt as if she would break. She now knew the pain of losing a child, and the cries of slave women mourning their lost and stolen children occupied her waking hours and haunted her dreams.

In March of 1850, Harriet determined she could no longer bear to mourn her own loss while so many others suffered in silence. She wrote to her friend, Gamaliel Bailey, who was the editor of an anti-slavery journal called *The National Era* and informed him that she planned to write a story about slavery. She said, "I feel now that the time is come when even a woman or a child who can speak a word for freedom and humanity is bound to speak... I hope every woman who can write will not be silent."

Just over a year later, the first installment of what would go on to become Stowe's most famous work, *Uncle Tom's Cabin*, was printed in *The National Era*. Installments continued weekly for just shy of a year, from June 5, 1851, to April 1, 1852 under the title, *Life Among the Lowly*, for which she was paid $400. *Uncle Tom's Cabin* was published in book form in March of 1852, and 5,000 copies were put into print. The copies sold out nearly immediately, and by the end of 1852, nearly 300,000 copies had been sold.

Her book shocked the world.

Northerners, previously ignorant to the savagery suffered by slaves at the hands of their masters and along trade routes from Africa, were appalled, and calls in the North for abolition reached a thunderous pitch. As copies of *Uncle Tom's Cabin* reached Europe, they were met with a similar response. No longer could free and God-fearing people say they didn't know of the plight of African slaves. *Uncle Tom's Cabin* showed how slavery touched all of society—not just slaves and traders and masters. It showed the humanness of slaves—something that few had ever considered—and described them as loyal friends, loving partners, and tender parents. It made every person in society an accomplice in the evils of this trade of human beings and demanded that they choose a side.

Harriet had hoped that her novel would help Southerners empathize with those they oppressed and perhaps even soften their hearts to the injustices suffered by many at their hands. But too much life and prosperity was tied up in the slaveholding culture of the antebellum South, and her work was met with indifference and offense there. Several people even tried to write books countering the claims made in *Uncle Tom's Cabin*. They painted a picture of benevolent masters and familial relationships between slaves and those who owned them and attempted to decry Stowe's account as inflammatory and exaggerated.

But Harriet had anticipated this, and in 1853 she released, *A Key to Uncle Tom's Cabin*, which contained all of the source material she had used to write her novel. The *Key* was full of documents and ledgers compiled by freed slaves, slave traders, and well-known abolitionists, and it supported with bare facts the atrocities presented in *Uncle Tom's Cabin*. When faced with glaring facts and supporting documentation, her detractors had little choice but to quietly disappear.

Former slave and fellow abolitionist Frederick Douglass wrote,

> But all efforts to conceal the enormity of slavery fail. The most unwise thing which, perhaps, was ever done by slaveholders, in order to hide the ugly features of slavery, was the calling in question, and denying the truthfulness of "*Uncle Tom's Cabin.*" They had better have owned the "soft impeachment" therein con-

tained—for the "KEY" not only proves the correctness of every essential part of "*Uncle Tom's Cabin*," but proves more and worse things against the murderous system than are alleged in that great book. Since the publication of that repository of human [*illegible*]—"*The Testimony of a Thousand Witnesses*"—there has not been an exposure of slavery so terrible as the *Key* to "Uncle Tom's Cabin." Let it be circulated far and wide, at home and abroad; let young and old read it, think of it, and learn from it to hate slavery with unappeasible intensity. The book, then, will be not only a *Key* to "Uncle Tom's Cabin," but a key to unlock the prison-house for the deliverance of millions who are now pining in chains, crying, "How LONG! HOW LONG! O LORD GOD! HOW LONG SHALL THESE THINGS BE?"

After the start of the Civil War, President Lincoln invited Harriet to visit him at the White House. Although little is known of this meeting, her son would later recount the words with which the president greeted Harriet. According to him, Lincoln tipped his tall black hat, put out his hand, and said, "So you are the little woman who wrote the book that started this great war."

Through the Lens of History

Sometimes, as time passes and cultures change, we look back at the way things once were and find ourselves shocked at the harshness or coarseness or ignorance with which our ancestors conducted themselves. Today, many people find *Uncle Tom's Cabin* offensive. They don't like the words that Harriet used—words that are now considered unacceptable to say. They don't like that Tom, a slave, showed loyalty and kindness to his master. They think that he would have been a better hero if he had been angrier and fought back against the institution and people that robbed him of his rightful freedom.

Sometimes the past makes us uncomfortable, and because we can, we consider that maybe it would be best if we simply didn't talk about it anymore and put out of sight the things that remind us of it. There have been many people who have wanted to put away *Uncle Tom's Cabin* and just not talk about it anymore. In the end, each person has to decide for themselves how they will view their history and the people and events that shaped it.

Regardless of how people today choose to see Harriet and her *Uncle Tom's Cabin*, it should be remembered that her work gave a voice to those who otherwise wouldn't have been heard. Her words touched the hearts of people who were previously unreachable. The truth she told about the evil institution of slavery changed its reputation forever, dealing it a cultural death-blow from which it would not recover.

Uncle Tom's Cabin changed the world for the better.

Her Mind Was Gone, but Her Spirit Remained

Harriet spent her years after *Uncle Tom's Cabin* lecturing on the evils of slavery, and in 1865, she saw its abolition with the passage of the 13th Amendment to the Constitution of the United States. She continued to fight for the underrepresented and those whose rights to life, liberty, and property were not duly represented and protected by government.

Her passion for writing never faded, and she would author over thirty books across a broad range of topics throughout her life. When her beloved Calvin died in the late summer of 1886, her health began to rapidly decline. Although she was still of sound body, her mind began to decay with what doctors today would call Alzheimer's disease.

Toward the end of her life, she set out again to write one last novel. Each day, she spent hours stooped over her desk, exhausting herself as she painstakingly put pen to paper composing her work. Friends and loved ones would sneak peeks at her manuscript only to find that she had begun rewriting *Uncle Tom's Cabin*, sometimes transcribing entire pages word for word from memory. She believed she was writing it for the first time and could not be dragged away from what she saw as this most important work.

Thankfully, she was surrounded by friends and family, who loved and looked after her and protected her physically and emotionally, taking care to never make her feel silly or confused, even though her behavior was sometimes very odd.

Her neighbors commonly left their doors open in the warm months to allow the breezes to freshen their homes, and they took it in stride when from seemingly nowhere, Harriet would appear in their drawing room at tea time or in the dining room for lunch. Sometimes, she got into mischief.

Among her patient neighbors was a man named Samuel Clements, a fellow author who was more commonly known as Mark Twain. In his autobiography, he recounted some of his memories of Harriet Beecher Stowe in the twilight years of her life:

> She wandered about all the day long in the care of a muscular Irish woman. Among the colonists of our neighborhood the doors always stood open in pleasant weather. Mrs. Stowe entered them at her own free will, and as she was always softly slippered and generally full of animal spirits, she was able to deal in surprises, and she liked to do it. She would slip up behind a person who was deep in dreams and musings and fetch a war whoop that would jump that person out of his clothes. And she had other moods. Sometimes we would hear gentle music in the drawing-room and would find her there at the piano singing ancient and melancholy songs with infinitely touching effect.

Harriet once wrote, "The bitterest tears shed over graves are for words left unsaid and deeds left undone." It's easy to imagine that Harriet lived her life with these words in mind. She seemed to see the whole world as her responsibility and endeavored to say and do all that she could with the time that she had in the hopes of leaving it better than she found it.

Harriet died on July 1st, 1896, and is buried next to Calvin and her son, Henry, in the historic cemetery at Phillips Academy. She was 85 years old.

Stephen
LANGTON

The Archbishop of Canterbury became the author of the Magna Carta, brokering a peace deal between an unpopular king and a group of rebel barons.

The Archbishop of Canterbury

In the 1200s, the King of England was revered in much the
same way as the pharaohs of ancient Egypt. A king was
believed to be all-powerful, predestined with authority to
rule over his people, and second in power only to God.
And so it was that when King John ascended to power
in 1199, after the death of his brother King Richard the
Lionheart, he felt no obligation to be particularly good,
or particularly fair, or particularly honest. His reign was
marked by conflict between him and the wealthy landown-
ers, called "barons," and the pope, who sat at the head of
the Catholic church.

John seemed to have trouble getting along with pretty
much everyone. As a young man, he had participated in
an uprising against his own father, and at various times
in his life, he sided either with or against each of his older
brothers in their attempts to gain the throne. Once, when
his brother King Richard was being held for ransom, John
and some of his friends actually offered to pay Richard's
captors to keep him so that John could steal the throne. Of
course, he didn't have a very good example growing up—
his own father had imprisoned John's mother when he was
only five years old!

The problem, it seemed, was that there just weren't really
any rules for royals, and so they behaved however they
wanted to.

When John finally did become king (his brother Richard
forgave him for trying to keep him in jail and steal the
throne and agreed to make him king after he died), his
rule was plagued by war with France and disagreements

with the barons as to how to get their land back. In those days, each time a country decided to go to war, they would have to build an army from scratch. The financial burden for the war fell to the people. Poor people had to send a member of their own family to fight in the war, and wealthy people could pay a tax instead of having to fight. Barons were kind of like governors or mayors, and they ruled over their own pieces of land, handling disagreements amongst the people who lived and worked on their land, but paid taxes to the king and had to fight his wars for him. The king needed the barons.

After suffering a devastating loss to France in 1214, the king tried to gain support for another war with the aim of reclaiming the land that France had taken, and he approached the barons in the hopes that they would agree to help him raise another army. But the barons were broke and battle-weary, and they didn't want to support John in another war with France.

At the same time, John was involved in a dispute with the pope that was beginning to turn ugly. The Archbishop of Canterbury had died in 1205, and John and the pope each felt entitled to pick the next Archbishop. The pope and the king argued back and forth for a couple of years, each appointing various people to the position, only to have the other dismiss them and replace them with their choice, until finally the pope played his most powerful card. He placed something called an "interdict" on the whole country of England, making it impossible for anyone in England to receive blessings and ordinances from the church. No baptisms, no funerals, no weddings, and no last rites.

King John was furious, and to get even, he closed all

churches in England and confiscated all of their wealth. The pope responded by excommunicating John and installing Stephen Langton as the Archbishop of Canterbury. John was powerless, and in 1213, he finally agreed to the pope's terms, ceding control of England to the church (who would still allow John to rule as king) and accepting Stephen Langton as the Archbishop.

Archbishop of the People

Stephen Langton was about fifteen years older than King John, but he had spent his life in pursuit of knowledge rather than chasing after power and land. Stephen had studied in Paris and was well versed in art, language, and history, as well as in scripture. He became quick friends with the pope, who admired his lively spirit and humble demeanor. Stephen was also an excellent orator and was known to captivate audiences when he spoke. The pope recognized in Stephen the potential to be a good and strong leader, which is why he had insisted on his placement as the Archbishop of Canterbury—a very powerful position in the church.

Stephen liked to think about the way that the Bible should influence people's everyday dealings with one another. He thought about the systems of government that worked, and the ones that didn't work, in the scriptures. He thought that since God had so much to say about how people should live their lives and treat one another, maybe God also had a preferred way for people to govern. He started thinking a lot about government and the way that a just and righteous king should lead, and he began asking questions of his audience when people would gather to hear him speak.

"What would you say," he would ask, "if a man were arrested simply because the king said that he had done something wrong?"

"Do you think that a man should be executed with only the testimony of the king against him, without having been tried in a court?" he would ask "And if a king did sentence someone to be executed, would the executioner be right to disobey the order of the king if he didn't believe that the accused deserved to die?"

No one had ever asked the people questions like these, and the people had, for the most part, never considered that the king might actually be just a person who should answer for his actions and have rules to live by just like anyone else. They had never thought that if a law wasn't a just law, then a person should be able to choose not to follow it.

Stephen wasn't trying to start an uprising. He believed that government could be good and that revolution was not the answer to dealing with a king who didn't think there should be limits to his power. Stephen was concerned with the righteousness of those who governed, and he wanted to help the people, not by starting a war but by establishing a form of government that put limits on the power of leaders and guaranteed rights to the people that no one could take away or ignore. Others had spoken of rights and had led uprisings and revolutions, but Stephen had something much more permanent—and much less bloody—in mind.

The Great Charter

The barons would prove to be the key to Langton's vision of a more just and accountable form of governance. Their weariness with the king's wars and his demands for more funding and more soldiers caused them to start looking for a leader who would better represent their interests. Allegiances were formed between the barons and a man named Robert Fitz Walter, who led them to London in May of 1215, where they publicly renounced their loyalty to the king. Forty barons and their armies marched with Robert—a mighty force to be sure—and at the end of the day, the barons and Robert held the city of London and its surrounding towns in their control.

Stephen saw this as his chance to bring about the reforms he felt his country needed in order to establish a more righteous government, and so he met privately and in secret with twenty-five barons and Robert Fitz Walter. At the center of Stephen's beliefs was the idea that the people should always be free to refuse to obey illegal and unjust laws and orders, and that people—all people, no matter how poor—should never be punished in any way without having the chance to be judged in a court by their equals. Stephen began drafting a document to offer to King John as a treaty to reestablish him as the rightful king but also to give the barons—and all other citizens of England—the rights and protections they deserved.

Ready for peace and a unification of his tattered kingdom, King John met the barons at Runnymede on the River Thames. Here, the barons and the archbishop laid out their terms. The king had suspected that Stephen and the barons wanted to steal the kingdom and rule for themselves, but what he found instead were a group of people who merely wanted the government to protect the rights of the people to live, prosper, and own their land. The charter demanded in clear language that the king be accountable for his actions and that his powers be limited to those which were just and right:

> No free man shall be seized or imprisoned, or stripped of his rights or possessions, or outlawed or exiled, or deprived of his standing in any other way, nor will we proceed with force against him, or send others to do so, except by the lawful judgement of his equals or by the law of the land. To no one will we sell, to no one deny or delay right or justice.

Unable to find cause to refuse the demands of the barons, King John signed the charter on June 15, 1215, and the barons submitted to his rule.

A Reference for Our Rights

A reading of the 1215 Magna Carta will probably sound familiar to most Americans. Much of the U.S. Constitution was heavily influenced by the Magna Carta and the words of Stephen Langton. His ponderings on the proper and limited role of government; the rights of people to assemble, own property, and pursue happiness in their lives; and their right to be free from unjust imprisonment and afforded due process under the law shaped much of the modern free world and influenced some of the greatest minds the world has known.

Benjamin Franklin summed up the influence of the Magna Carta well when he spoke of "A government of laws, and not of men." He, like Stephen Langton 500 years before, understood this to mean that no man was above natural law and that all men—even kings and presidents—are equal under law, and no leader or government could do things that those subject to their rule could not.

Prudence
CRANDALL

As an educated woman herself, Prudence opened her own school in 1831 to teach girls. Her decision to admit a black girl led to violence from neighbors, arrest, and time in jail—but she remained devoted to teaching African-American girls.

A Hero for Education

It's hard to believe that there was once a time when many adults thought it was okay to yell and cuss and throw rocks or rotten food at little children as they walked home from school, or that in many towns, simply believing that all people were equal and should be treated with respect and kindness and love could cause a person to lose all that they had worked hard for—or even to fear for their life—but that is just what people like Prudence Crandall faced in the early part of the twentieth century.

Prudence was born into a farming family in Rhode Island in 1803. When she was ten years old, her family moved to Canterbury, Connecticut. The Crandalls were Quakers, and that meant that they believed in equal education opportunities for men and women, and also in being kind and gentle to all people. Prudence's parents enrolled her in the New England Friends' Boarding school in Providence where she was privileged to learn many subjects that most women of her

time weren't commonly taught. Latin, math, and science filled Prudence's mind, and her youth and early adulthood saw her grow in knowledge of the world around her and in good and gentle works towards her fellowman.

Prudence loved learning and helping others so much that she decided to become a teacher. She was very good at teaching, and soon she left her job in order to open her very own school. Word quickly spread throughout the region. Ms. Crandall's school quickly became known as one of the best in New England! Because girls and boys didn't go to school together in those days, many wealthy families sent their daughters to study under Prudence's capable hand. Her curriculum was demanding and she expected greatness from all of her students. Many people said that Ms. Crandall's school was just as fine—if not finer—than any of the best boys' academies in the state.

When Prudence was twenty-nine she invited Sarah Harris, a young black woman from a wealthy family, to come study at her school. Sarah hoped to become a teacher, so she knew that she had to learn from the best! Many white families in Canterbury were angry that their children were attending the same school as a black student. They demanded that Prudence expel Sarah immediately! But Sarah would not be bullied into treating someone unfairly—she would not bow to the demands of people filled with ignorance and hate. She told the families of her students that she would continue to teach *all* students who had come to her school to learn.

Miss Crandall's School for Young Ladies and Little Misses of Color

Prudence knew what could happen if the angry parents continued to demand that she expel Sarah. She said, "The school may fail, but I will not give up Sarah Harris." Prudence understood that if she continued to teach Sarah, the parents of her white students might pull them out of her school—leaving her without a way to earn a living and do what she loved best. But she also knew that she had to do what was right.

Sure enough, one by one, the white families brought their daughters home from Ms. Crandall's school. Soon, only Prudence and Sarah Harris were left.

Never one to be discouraged for too long, Prudence made a plan. One day, a new sign appeared outside the school. It read: Miss Crandall's School for Young Ladies and Little Misses of Color. The treatment of Sarah Harris by the parents of her students helped her to see how difficult it was for black girls to get a quality education, and so she became the first black girls' school in Connecticut.

Sarah sought the counsel of Samuel J. May and William Lloyd Garrison, two prominent abolitionists, and they helped spread the word. On April 1, 1833, twenty girls and young women arrived from five different states to take up residence as full-time students at Ms. Crandall's school. Many of the townspeople were enraged! It was bad enough that she had allowed Sarah Harris to learn at her school—now she was bringing in black students from all over New England!

Some people feared that the presence of Ms. Crandall's school would cause people to think that black people were equal with white people—they were afraid that white men might want to marry black women, and they hated that idea!

Every day, when Ms. Crandall's students left school property, townspeople followed them—taunting them with ugly racial slurs, and throwing eggs and rocks and rotten food at them. It seemed that everywhere they turned they were met with anger, hatred and persecution. Prudence and her students remained steadfast in their cause. All people deserved a chance to learn and to better themselves, and the screams and jeers of angry bigots would not make that any less true.

Prudence's neighbor, Andrew Judson happened to be a lawyer and the state of Connecticut's most well-loved politician. Judson hated Ms. Crandall's school and made it his personal mission to see it closed. He said:

> We are not merely opposed to the establishment of that school in Canterbury; we mean there shall not be such a school set up anywhere in our State. The colored people can never rise from their menial condition in our country; they ought not to be permitted to rise here. They are an inferior race of beings, and never can or ought to be recognized as the equals of the whites.

In the spring of 1833, Judson got what he wanted. The state of Connecticut passed the "Black Law" which prohibited schools from teaching black students from a different state without the express consent of the community. Prudence was undeterred. She kept teaching.

The townspeople refused to serve Prudence or her students at any of the local establishments. It was also hard for them to get food or clothing or medical attention because none of the shops would let them buy the things they needed. Stage drivers refused to transport them, and doctors refused to treat them when they were sick or injured. Even all the churches except Prudence's refused to let them worship. One night, townspeople poisoned the well—the only source of water for the school—by filling it with animal feces.

In July, Prudence was arrested and thrown in jail.

At her trial, the jury had a difficult time deciding if Prudence was guilty or not, and a second trial was held in which the state finally succeeded in getting the "guilty" verdict they were hoping for. Later, a higher court overturned the conviction, and Prudence continued to teach.

Moving On

Although she had won the legal battle—and perhaps *because* she had won—the persecution from the town of Canterbury became unbearable for Prudence and her students. The windows in the school were destroyed, angry mobs set the school on fire, and all of the furniture was damaged beyond repair. It was only a matter of time before a student might be seriously injured or killed. Finally, on September 10, 1834, Miss Crandall's School for Young Ladies and Little Misses of Color closed its doors for the last time. Prudence was unwilling to risk the lives of her students in a town so full of ignorance and hate.

After closing the school and marrying a fellow abolition-ist and minister named Calvin Philleo, Prudence decided that it was time to leave Connecticut. She stayed long enough to see the Black Law repealed in 1838. Secure in the knowledge that she had done what she could to protect the right to education for young black women, she and her husband moved to Illinois and Prudence opened another school, this time free of the threats and persecution she had faced in her home state.

When her husband died, Prudence moved one more time to live with her brother in Kansas.

In 1886, with heavy encouragement by the writer Mark Twain, the Connecticut legislature voted to give Ms. Crandall an annual pension of $400 (about $11,000 today). Prudence died in Elk Falls, Kansas, at the age of 86. On October 1, 1995, Prudence was named the state heroine of the state of Connecticut.

Today, Miss Crandall's School for Young Ladies and Misses of Color is called the Prudence Crandall Museum. It stands as a testament to the sacrifice of one woman and her twenty students who fought for education and equality in the face of ignorance, hate, and violence.

To me the trail is calling! The old trail, the trail that is always new.

Matthew
HENSON

Forging a new path to the North Pole,
Henson spent years on dangerous
expeditions in the Arctic and later became
the first African-American to be made a life
member of The Explorers Club.

The First Explorer to Reach the North Pole

In the year 1909, a group of six men traveling on dog sleds made their way through the frozen arctic wilderness. They traveled four hundred and thirteen nautical miles, all the way to the North Pole. Many people were suspicious of the explorers' story. They doubted that an American flag had actually been planted at the northernmost point of the globe, and for a long time, people believed a lie about who actually arrived there first. But time has a way of bringing the truth to light, and now we know what really happened.

The first person to ever stand on the top of the world was a black man named Matthew Henson.

Life at Sea

Matthew Alexander Henson was born in the late summer of the year 1866 to a family of sharecroppers in Maryland. It had only been one year since slavery had been abolished, and as one of the first black men to walk freely in the United States, Matthew led a life of exploration and discovery that few before him had enjoyed. His spirit was free, and his appetite for adventure was insatiable.

Matthew faced many trials early in life. Orphaned by the age of ten, he made his own way in the world and developed an abnormal fearlessness and tenacity. He wasn't afraid of hard work, and he wasn't afraid to take big risks; he knew his life was his to live, and he resolved from a young age to live it to its fullest. When he was nearly eleven, he gathered with a large crowd to hear former slave

Frederick Douglass give a speech. Douglass challenged black people to work hard to gain an education and to challenge themselves to be independent and strong in character and body. Matthew was inspired by Douglass's words, and they helped shape the way he would choose to live his life from then on.

When he was only twelve, Matthew signed up to be a cabin boy aboard a ship named the *Katie Hines* and would sail for the next six years under the mentorship of Captain Childs. Matthew would receive an education at the hand of his captain. Childs dedicated part of each day to teaching his young apprentice to read and write. He also encouraged Matthew to learn how to do other jobs on the ship, so that with each passing year, Matthew's skills and abilities increased. Matthew and Captain Childs sailed the world together for nine years. They visited China, Africa, and Japan and even explored the Black Sea! When Captain Childs passed away in 1887, 21-year-old Henson left the *Katie Hines* and set sail on a new adventure, this time as a shop clerk in Washington, D.C.

Peary and Henson

Although his time at sea was a thing of the past, Matthew still dreamed of a life of adventure. And so when a twist of fate brought a naval officer into the shop where Matthew was working to sell seal and walrus skins he had collected on an expedition to Greenland, Matthew confidently pitched his abilities and experience in the hopes of being invited on the explorer's next adventure. Impressed with Matthew's vast experience and his enthusiasm for life,

Robert Peary hired him on the spot. Matthew left his job as a shop clerk and took his place as Peary's personal assistant. They began planning their first adventure together.

Peary was serving in the Navy Corps of Civil Engineers and had been tasked with mapping and exploring the jungles of Nicaragua, in the hopes of finding a route suitable for a canal to connect the Atlantic Ocean to the Pacific. Matthew spent the next two years traveling through rainforests in Central America with Peary. The trip cemented their friendship and formed the bonds that would keep them together for the next 23 years, 18 of which would be spent on expeditions to the farthest corners of the world.

Together, they created the first complete map of Greenland and were the first to visit the island's northernmost point. There, they recovered three massive fragments of meteor that they would sell to the American Museum of Natural History for $40,000. The largest piece, called the Cape York meteorite, was the third-largest meteor ever to be found and the heaviest ever to be transported by human beings. It weighed a whopping 34 tons! Peary and Henson dragged it all the way from Greenland to the American Museum of Natural History, where it is still on display today. The money the partners obtained from the sale of the meteors would go on to support their expeditions for the next ten years.

Although Peary was the face the public knew—it was unheard of in those days for black men to be credited as equals with whites—Matthew was in charge in the field. He was a talented carpenter and personally built and maintained all the sleds the team used on their wintry explorations. Matthew was also fluent in the Inuit language and established friendships with the native people of the region. He was known as "Matthew the Kind One," a good example of how a man can be strong, brave, and powerful, yet also gentle and kind. Matthew was humble and learned all that he could from the people he encountered on his travels. His Inuit friends taught him all the ways they had learned to survive and travel in the hostile and dangerous frozen North. "He was more of an Eskimo than some of them," Peary once remarked.

Matthew was an accomplished fisherman, hunter, and dog handler, and it was he who took responsibility for training everyone who joined their expeditions. Even the most experienced men in their company had much to learn from Matthew.

The team would try and fail many times to reach the North Pole. Each time they were forced to turn back, they congratulated themselves for having made it farther than they had the last time, and each time they gave thanks for the safety of themselves and their crew. They knew how dangerous their work was, and they counted themselves blessed each time they returned home without injury or loss of life. In 1906, with the help of an ice-breaker gifted to them by President Theodore Roosevelt, they made it within 175 miles of the pole before inclement weather forced them to turn back once more.

One Last Time

Two years later, the friends set out on their eighth and final attempt to reach the Pole. Whether they succeeded or not—both men were now in their forties and were beginning to feel the effects of their long and strenuous careers—they had come to the decision that their eighth expedition would be their last together. Once again aboard their ship, the *Roosevelt*, the large, hand-picked crew of elite explorers and survivalists set out for adventure. This time, they had a new strategy, one that Henson and Peary were optimistic would bring them their long-awaited success. They intended to ferry and deposit loads of gear and food along the way, setting up caches of supplies along their route. Each team would then return to the ship, which would be iced into port on Ellesmere Island. The final team would consist of just Peary and Henson and four Inuit guides, who would—in theory—be able to travel between supply checkpoints and make it to the Pole well fed and well rested. Peary believed that he could never make the trek without his dear friend. "Henson must go all the way, I can't make it there without him," he wrote in his diary.

Along the way they were met with constant trials, such as cracking and drifting ice that formed patches of open water known as "leads," and temperatures recorded at sixty-five degrees below freezing. In Matthew's firsthand account, *The Negro at the North Pole*, a book published in 1912, he detailed a summary of the five-day march from their last supply stop to the Pole. Henson, Peary, and the four Inuit men accompanying them, Ooqueah, Ootah, Egingwah, and Seeglo, drove the five remaining dog teams at an incredible pace day after day, for stretches that lasted between twelve and fourteen hours at a time. They moved quickly in the hopes that they would avoid leads opening up behind them, breaking their path and making it impossible to return the way they had come. Every mile of their journey was full of risk.

"We crawled out of our igloos and found a dense mist hanging over everything," Matthew wrote in his book. "Only at intervals, when the sun's rays managed to penetrate the mist, could we catch even a glimpse of the sky. Estimating the distance that we had come during the last four days, we figured that, unless something unusual happened to us during the course of this day, we should be at the Pole before its close."

Peary had grown fatigued, and accounts from the journey indicate that he may have been suffering frostbite on some of his toes. Resting in one of the sleds, he sent Matthew ahead to scout the trail. Finding it free of leads and safe for travel, he returned to Peary, and they set out to meet their goal. Matthew spent much of the journey in the lead sled. "The Commander, who was about fifty yards behind, called out to me and said we would go into camp," Matthew wrote. "We were in good spirits, and none of us were cold. So we went to work and promptly built our igloos, fed our dogs and had dinner. The sun being obscured by the mist, it was impossible to make observations and tell whether or not we had actually reached the Pole. The only thing we could do was to crawl into our igloos and go to sleep."

The next morning, with the mist clearing, they set out to travel what they thought would be the last few miles of their journey. But when Peary took measurements of their location in relativity to the position of the sun during midday, they realized they had actually *passed* the Pole by a short distance. They turned around and retraced their steps, ending up back at their camp.

"The results of the first observation showed that we had

figured out the distance very accurately, for when the flag was hoisted over the geographical center of the Earth it was located just behind our igloos," recalled Matthew.

Two Different Tales of Discovery

But who had arrived first? Matthew wrote, "I was in the lead that had overshot the mark by a couple of miles, we went back then and I could see that my footprints were the first at the spot." Because he had been sent to scout ahead, Matthew Henson had left the first human footprints at the North Pole. But sometimes, what *really* happens gets lost— or purposely omitted—in the retelling of adventures, and so it was in the case of the Peary/Henson discovery of the Pole. Something changed the moment Peary saw Henson's footprints in the snow.

Things were never the same between the men again.

After the party's return to the United States, many news articles would imply a strain between Peary and Henson over who had reached the North Pole first. "From the time we knew we were at the Pole, Commander Peary scarcely spoke to me," Matthew would later say. "It nearly broke my heart ... that he would rise in the morning and slip away on the homeward trail without rapping on the ice for me, as was the established custom."

It seems strange that after a long and happy friendship, Peary would turn cold toward Henson in the very moment of their success. They had, after all, been on the same expedition, and when considering the years of work that had gone into arriving at the Pole, it seemed silly to consider the arrival of Henson at the spot an hour or so before Peary as anything of any real consequence. Why couldn't they have just claimed arrival together and shared in the glory of their accomplishment?

Away from the world, alone with their dogs and their Inuit guides, Henson and Peary had always been equals—friends and explorers whose lives depended on each other—but the world they faced upon return to the United States was not one that welcomed equality and friendship between blacks and whites. The world didn't want a black hero-explorer, and for reasons only he understood, Peary gave them what they wanted. He received all recognition as the man who discovered the North Pole while Matthew was reduced to nothing more than Peary's "trusty companion" in the accounts that even bothered to mention him. All of Matthew's value and contribution was sidelined and ignored, as Peary was paraded around the country as a national hero.

Robert Peary died on February 20, 1920. Upon returning home from their expedition, he had been promoted to Rear Admiral in the U.S. Navy and spent his final years traveling the world, dining with world leaders and speaking of his accomplishments, content, it seemed, to allow Matthew and his contributions and accomplishments to simply fade away.

After returning from the North Pole, Matthew was given a job as a clerk with the Federal Customs House in New York City. He would spend the next thirty years of his life in relative seclusion. He married a woman named Lucy, but they had no children.

Finally, in 1937, Matthew's contributions would begin to come to light. He was contacted by the Explorers Club of New York, who recognized him as an honorary member. A couple of years after Matthew's induction into the Explorers Club, he received an award—identical to the one awarded to Peary—by the United States Navy, and in the year 1954, at the age of 87, Matthew was invited to the White House by President Dwight Eisenhower to receive a special commendation for his previous work as an explorer on the behalf of the United States of America.

Matthew Henson passed away the following year on March 9, 1955. He was buried in Woodlawn Cemetery in the Bronx, New York, but in 1988, under the direction of President Ronald Reagan, his remains were moved, along with his wife's, to Arlington National Cemetery. On the 79th anniversary of his having reached the North Pole, Henson was laid to rest with full military honors near the monument to Robert Peary. In 1996, an oceanographic survey ship was commissioned as the U.S.N.S *Henson* in his honor, and in 2000, the National Geographic Society presented Henson posthumously with its most esteemed award, the Hubbard Medal.

Ironically, the first recipient of this prize was Robert Peary, in 1906.

Laura and Rose
WILDER

A mother and daughter duo most famous
for Laura's *Little House* book series, The
Wilder women were eloquent advocates
for self-reliance and freedom.

Lovers of Liberty and Little Houses on Prairies

Rose Wilder Lane didn't have much love in her heart for South Dakota. In fact, she once wrote, "I hated everything and everybody in my childhood with such bitterness and resentment that I didn't want to remember anything about it."

Thankfully, however, Rose *did* remember. Her mother, Laura, remembered too, and the memories of the famous mother and daughter combined to create stories of life on the American frontier and of the hard years their family endured. Those years were full of hardships that drove Laura and her family away from their beloved home in the Big Woods of Wisconsin; hardships that saw Rose accidentally set fire to the family home—causing her parents to lose everything they had; and hardships of the Great Depression and the loss of everything—again! Laura and Rose suffered much throughout their lives, but they also experienced great joy, and their ability to weave stories of life and loss and suffering and joy entertained and inspired generations—reminding all who read their stories of the importance of surviving the hard things, finding the good in everyday life, and writing down the things that are important.

Roses Can Bloom in the Hardest of Places

Rose Wilder was born in the cold and bitter of early December, 1886. Her mother, Laura Ingalls Wilder, named her little daughter for the prairie rose that blooms pink and fragrant across the rugged frontier, because Laura believed "she symbolized a hope and longing," and she hoped that in naming her little girl Rose "all of Dakota could be as flowerful as the mass of wild roses that covered the land during the month of June."

Laura gave birth in a tiny house just north of De Smet, South Dakota. Laura and her husband would have a son a couple of years later, but he would only live twelve days and die without a name. Heartbroken, the Wilders wouldn't have more children and instead devoted their love and attention to young Rose.

By the time Rose was born, her parents, Almanzo and Laura Wilder, were already deep in debt. The family had lost their entire crop to a massive hail storm that destroyed the whole wheat harvest. Just one year after the family's crops had failed, Laura and Almanzo became ill with diphtheria, an infection that attacks the heart and can cause paralysis and death. Although Laura would make a full recovery and Rose would be spared, Almanzo was weakened and left partially paralyzed. He would eventually improve, but would have to use a cane for the rest of his life.

Moving, and Moving Some More

Although Almanzo had once been relatively prosperous, bad luck and unexpected difficulties proved to be his lot in life. As a result, he often had to move his family to follow work or take refuge with relatives when times got really bad. The Wilders lived with Almanzo's family in Spring Valley, Minnesota, for a time and then moved to the southeastern United States, on the Florida panhandle, to help work the farm of Rose's great-uncle Peter. They had hoped that the warmer weather would be easier on Almanzo, but despite the beautiful scenery and intriguing wildlife, they failed to make a home there either. Leaving muggy Florida, they headed back to South Dakota just in time to be in the very thick of the Panic of 1893 an economic depression that lasted for four years.

Rolling the dice one more time, hoping that their luck would finally improve, Laura, Rose, and Almanzo set their course for Missouri. They named their farm Rocky Ridge, and in the little ramshackle cabin, they finally put down roots.

Although life was still hard, they found a measure of prosperity at Rocky Ridge. Having learned from their mistakes in the Dakota Territory, they diversified their investment, planting various crops, as well as establishing a large apple orchard and a dairy farm, and raising hogs and chickens. Never again would they be dependent on only one source of income. Rocky Ridge provided the stability the family had longed for, and Laura and Almanzo slept well at night for the first time, their futures secure and their bellies full.

Blooming

As Rose grew, she longed for a faster paced life away from the small farm towns she'd always called home. She wanted adventure and thought of nothing but stepping out into the big world on her own. As a compromise, her parents agreed to let her move to Crowley, Louisiana, a relatively large town, where her aunt, Almanzo's quirky and well-traveled sister, Eliza Jane, lived.

In Eliza, Rose found a kindred spirit, and she treasured the years she spent with her. Rose attended high school, where she set herself apart from her peers with her quick wit, bright mind, and exceptional intellect. Her teachers were impressed with her writing and her mastery of Latin, a course that should have taken her three years to complete but which she managed to condense into one! While in school, Rose took an interest in politics and became endeared to Eugene Debs, the founder of the Socialist Party of America and five-time failed presidential candidate. Rose worked briefly on one of his campaigns, but the socialist message of "fairness for all" and a government that provided for the needs of the people took hold in Rose's young mind. She knew the suffering of poverty and the effect it had on individuals and families. She remembered all too well being the "poor kid" at school without new books or new clothes like the other students. She felt a burning resentment for those who seemed to simply have more than others, and she didn't think it was right for people to suffer the unfairness of inequality.

Upon graduating from high school and unable to afford college, Rose decided to informally study under the experienced father of one of her classmates, who taught her telegraphy at their local train station. Still not even eighteen years old, Rose moved to Kansas City, where she found work with the Western Union. Rose spent the next five years working all over the United States, trying her hand at selling real estate in California, working in telegraphy throughout the Midwest, and—most importantly—writing all along the way.

Back at Rocky Ridge, Almanzo had purchased a typewriter for his wife in the hopes that she would begin to write as well. In 1908, Rose published her very first piece in a newspaper called the *San Francisco Call* and joined her father in encouraging her mother to write. Rose had read her mother's handwritten journals, crammed full of her childhood adventures with her prairie-settling family, and she felt her mother had enough talent to supplement the family income if she took up writing.

Laura listened to her daughter, and while Rose was writing unconventional articles for the *Kansas City Post*—including one about a hen, obviously influenced by Halley's Comet, that had laid an egg with a meteorically long tail—Laura published her first piece under the pen name Mrs. A.J. Wilder. It was a piece titled "Profits of the Good Fat Hen," and it was met with positive response from readers of the local farming magazine.

No matter that they were both writing about chickens—the Wilder women were both published writers!

Finding Their Way

By the time Rose was 28, she was married and working at the *San Francisco Bulletin*. She progressed quickly from editing the words of others to writing her own column under her own name and photo. In those days, newspapers published everything—fiction, nonfiction, news stories, opinion pieces—and Rose did it all! She had such a talent for writing that her work began to appear in other newspapers around the country. She was a national name!

Despite her professional success, Rose's home life was not a happy one. She and her husband, Claire Lane, had suffered heartbreak at the start of their marriage with the stillbirth of their son. A subsequent surgery likely left Rose unable to bear children, and she and Claire began to grow apart.

In 1915, Laura traveled to San Francisco to stay with Rose and Claire and attend the Panama-Pacific International Exposition—a world's fair to celebrate the completion of the Panama Canal that featured the most exciting modern inventions and food from around the world. They even ran a telephone line from San Francisco all the way to New York so that people on the East Coast could have a chance to hear the sound of the Pacific Ocean! Laura, having spent all of her life in rural America, was wide-eyed with wonder at all the new sights, sounds, and tastes. She was so moved by the experience that she wrote often to her husband, detailing all the excitement of her trip. Her letters were published after her death in a book called *West from Home*.

Although the visit was a wild success for Laura, it marked the end of Rose and Claire's marriage. They separated on good terms, however, and went their separate ways—although Rose did keep Claire's last name for the remainder of her life. Near the time she ended her marriage, she left the newspaper to strike out on her own as a freelance writer.

Politics

Although a socialist in her youth, by the time she was in her early thirties, Rose had aligned with the views of Karl Marx and identified herself as a communist. She believed that communism was the surest way to provide fair opportunities and equality to people on a large scale. Part of her freelance work saw her traveling around post-WWI

Europe with the American Red Cross, documenting the things she saw. While there, she spent significant time in countries that had implemented communism. For the first time, Rose saw her ideology in practice. She was horrified and later recalled,

> I came out of the Soviet Union no longer a communist, because I believed in personal freedom. Like all Americans, I took for granted the individual liberty to which I had been born. It seemed as necessary and as inevitable as the air I breathed; it seemed the natural element in which human beings lived. What I saw was not an extension of human freedom, but the establishment of tyranny on a new, widely extended and deeper base.

Cured of communism, Rose returned to the United States and began writing about the power and sanctity of the individual. She spoke critically of government overreach and corruption and sought out like-minded men and women to share her thoughts with. She began friendships with Ayn Rand and Isabel Paterson, and the three became literary powerhouses for what would become the libertarian movement. Lane, Rand, and Paterson are known today as the mothers of libertarianism and Albert Jay Nock would claim that they wrote "the only intelligible books on the philosophy of individualism that have been written in America this century" and that they had "shown the male world of this period how to think fundamentally. [...] [T]hey don't fumble and fiddle around – every shot goes straight to the centre."

As Rose focused more on her political writing, Laura was working on a project that would change both of their lives. A handwritten manuscript full of stories of Wisconsin and of making butter and pork cracklins in log cabins in the Big Woods was beginning to take shape. Laura asked Rose to help with the editing, and the mother and daughter team brought to life the story of the Ingalls family—Ma, Pa, Laura, Caroline, Mary, and Grace. *The Little House in the Big Woods* was published in 1932 and immediately catapulted Laura Ingalls Wilder to fame.

She was 65 years old.

Laura and Rose continued to collaborate for the rest of Laura's life. They went on to author eight *Little House* books together and collaborated on countless other projects. They took care to weave messages of individualism, self-reliance, and merit-based reward into the *Little House* series, using their popularity and influence to help spread and promote messages of liberty.

Rose would continue to travel the world and write about her experiences. She died in her sleep at age 81 on October 30, 1968—having planned to begin a three-year world tour the next day.

Little Rock
NINE

Selected by the NAACP for their good grades and attendance, these high school students were asked to stand up for their rights and insist on attending a racially segregated government school.

Preparing for a Fight

Not too very long ago, there were nine teenagers who were asked to do something very important, very dangerous, and very brave.

They weren't asked to swim with sharks, or climb a mountain, or walk a tightrope across a canyon, or rush into a burning building to save a kitten. They weren't asked to fight a giant, or wrestle an alligator, or negotiate a peace deal between two countries. No, what they were asked to do was even more dangerous, more scary, and more important than any of those things.

These nine special teenagers were asked to go to school.

And for the United States of America, Melba Pattillo, Ernest Green, Elizabeth Eckford, Minnijean Brown, Terrence Roberts, Carlotta Walls, Jefferson Thomas, Gloria Ray, and Thelma Mothershed going to school was one of the most important things that would ever happen.

It was also the scariest and most dangerous thing that many of them would ever do.

Brown vs. Board of Education

It sounds crazy now, but not very long ago—in fact, there are many people still alive today who remember it—the law prevented white people and black people from doing many things together. They couldn't ride the bus together (the black people had to sit at the back of the bus, while the white people got to sit at the front); they couldn't use the same public restrooms (there were signs above the doors that said "FOR WHITES ONLY" and "COLORED"); they couldn't drink from the same drinking fountains; they couldn't sit in the same restaurants; they couldn't go to the same movie theaters, be treated in the same hospitals, or sit in the same section of the public library.

And they couldn't go to school together.

Things had been this way for almost as long as anyone could remember—since 1896, when the Supreme Court ruled that black people and white people should be "separate but equal." This ruling led to what became known as "Jim Crow" laws, which created separate spaces for black people and white people to do things in public. The ruling said that segregating people based on the color of their skin was okay, as long as black people's facilities were just as nice as white people's. But even that rule was not obeyed. In fact, the restrooms, theaters, hospitals, schools, and other public and private places that black people had to use were often in such disrepair and functioned so poorly that they were hardly usable. But because white politicians controlled all the money and white people ran most of the businesses, it was very difficult for black people to make things better for themselves.

They were living in the "Land of the Free" but were unable to find a working public restroom when they needed one and were treated as if they were less than whites, simply because of the color of their skin.

Something had to change. And finally, in 1954, something did: the U.S. Supreme Court—the highest court in the land—decided that it was unconstitutional to force black children to go to different schools than white children.

In some areas of the country, the new ruling was well received. A lot of people realized that segregation (separating people according to race) was wrong, and they believed the words in the Declaration of Independence:

> We hold these truths to be self-evident, that *all men are created equal*, that they are endowed by their Creator with certain unalienable Rights, that among these are Life, Liberty and the Pursuit of Happiness.

They knew that people who were judged by the color of their skin—and given fewer rights because of it—were not being treated equally and that their rights to life, liberty, and the pursuit of happiness were not being protected by the government, and they began to make changes.

Some states, like Missouri, West Virginia, Kentucky, Oklahoma, and Maryland, did a pretty good job at desegregating schools, and the integration of black and white students went smoothly.

But in other places, things did not go well at all.

September 4, 1957

Orval Faubus, the Governor of Arkansas, did not like desegregation. He feared that allowing Arkansas schools to follow the new Supreme Court ruling would harm his chances of being reelected. He didn't want to risk angering his fellow members of the Southern Democrat party, who did not like the idea of black people being given the same rights and privileges as whites.

Governor Faubus and his friend and fellow Southern

Democrat, James Johnson, devised a tricky plan to keep black students from attending school without openly defying the Supreme Court ruling. They knew that they could use fear to get people to do what they wanted, so they started spreading rumors that an angry mob of white people was going to come to the school and instigate violence against the students as they entered. No mob was actually coming, but they talked about it enough that the people began to worry.

Once people started worrying, the governor and his friend had them right where they wanted them and were able to propose a solution to the very "problem" they had created!

The Governor used his authority to call up the National Guard and stationed armed soldiers all around the school. He told the people that this show of force was to protect the students from the "angry mob" that was coming, but the soldiers told a different story. According to them, they were under orders to form a barricade and keep the students from entering the school.

The Little Rock Nine

Nine brave teenagers had been carefully selected to be the first to integrate into Central High school in Little Rock, Arkansas. They all had excellent grades and perfect attendance. They were model students who had set themselves apart as the best and brightest of their peers. After spending most of their school years in poor black schools, they were excited to see what opportunities for learning and advancement awaited them at their new school.

As they walked toward Central High School that early autumn morning, they were met with a harrowing sight.

They had been warned that there would be many people—students and staff—who wouldn't want them there. They knew that the Governor didn't want them there. They had been carefully prepared for the hardships they were likely to face and had been given important advice: don't get angry no matter what people say to you; don't fight back if someone pushes you; don't give them a reason to hate you.

Just put your head up, and keep walking.

And that's what they tried to do.

But as they got closer, the crowd grew louder. A line of soldiers with guns stood shoulder to shoulder, blocking the entrance to the school. A barrage of rocks and garbage, as well as ugly words and racial slurs, were hurled at the courageous students.

Elizabeth Eckford later wrote about the experience:

> They moved closer and closer. ... Somebody started yelling. ... I tried to see a friendly face somewhere in the crowd—someone who maybe could help. I looked into the face of an old woman and it seemed a kind face, but when I looked at her again, she spat on me.

Governor Faubus had succeeded in. He had mixed fear and racism to create the very mob he claimed to be trying to protect against. The nine brave teenagers would not be entering the school today.

Eisenhower and the 101st

After weeks of protests and as the National Guard continued to bar the students from entering their school, President Eisenhower called a meeting with Governor Faubus. He secured a promise from the governor that he would cease blocking the integration of Central High School. When the governor went back on his word, President Eisenhower federalized the National Guard—effectively taking control of the Arkansas state militia.

He also activated the United States Army's famous 101st Airborne Division and sent them to surround the school, along with the members of the Arkansas National Guard, who had a new mission: Protect the nine brave students from the crowd, and see them safely into their school.

And so it was that by the end of September, 1957, Melba, Ernest, Elizabeth, Minnijean, Terrence, Carlotta, Jefferson, Gloria, and Thelma were officially the first black students at Central High School.

But their troubles were hardly over. Most of them were mistreated every single day.

Minnijean was expelled after she finally dumped a bowl of chili on top of some young men who were ruthlessly harassing her in the lunchroom. Melba Patillo had acid thrown into her eyes and was locked in a bathroom stall, while a group of white girls stood in the neighboring stall and dropped flaming pieces of paper down on her.

Fighting a Losing Battle

And still, the governor fought desegregation.

By the end of summer, 1958, Governor Faubus had devised a new plan. He reasoned that although the President had kept him from keeping the black students out of the schools, he didn't have the authority to force the governor to actually open the schools. And so, just as schools in Arkansas were preparing for the new school year, the Governor ordered all four public high schools in Little Rock to close indefinitely. His plan was to reopen them as private schools, since the Supreme Court ruling only applied to public schools. It seemed he was willing to stop at nothing to keep racist and archaic policies of segregation in place.

But good has a way of winning out in the end, and the Little Rock School Board voted out their segregationist members and replaced them with people who believed in the fair treatment of black students. The governor's plan to privatize the schools failed also, and by the summer of 1959, Faubus had run out of options. Schools opened to both black and white students on August 12, 1959.

A Legacy

The 1958-1959 school year became known as "The Lost Year"—when black and white high school students in an American city were at the mercy of those who refused to believe that all people were deserving of equal treatment under the law. The divisions and bad feelings caused by the events of The Lost Year had a lasting effect and shaped the future of desegregation across much of the south.

School attendance didn't get any easier for the Little Rock Nine. They sacrificed years that should have been full of camaraderie and happiness in order to pave the way for others. They suffered humiliation, physical attacks, verbal abuse, and every imaginable plot to run them off and make them too afraid to go to school. But they persevered, and their bravery laid a foundation for other brave men and women who fought in the battle for civil rights.

Children today can thank the Little Rock Nine for the surprise and shock they feel when they learn that one of the bravest things a black teenager in 1957 could do was go to school. If it hadn't been for the Little Rock Nine, who knows how long men and women like Governor Orval Faubus would have maintained control over cities and states around the country? Who knows how long children in the Land of the Free would have missed out on the chance to have friends and loved ones of all different ethnicities and backgrounds?

We all owe a debt of gratitude to the brave young men and women who faced great fear and danger to do something brave and important.

In 1999, President Bill Clinton awarded the Little Rock Nine the Congressional Gold Medal—the highest award given to civilians by the government of the United States. It is given to those "who have performed an achievement that has an impact on American history and culture that is likely to be recognized as a major achievement in the recipient's field long after the achievement."

The Congressional Gold Medal has only been awarded 163 times in its 244-year history. The first recipient of the award was General George Washington in 1776.

Melba Pattillo grew up in a family that valued education and knowledge. Her mother, Lois Marie Pattillo, earned her PhD in English at the University of Arkansas in 1954, being one of the very first black graduates from the school. Melba attended Horace Mann High School in Little Rock and realized that the quality of education there was nowhere near the pedigree of education the white students at Central High were receiving, so when the opportunity to attend Central arose, she was quick to volunteer. After a year of attending Central High, she moved to California, where she lived with foster parents in order to finish her high school career at Montgomery High School in Santa Rosa, California. She went on to earn a master's degree in journalism at Columbia University and a doctorate in education at the University of San Francisco. She is currently the Chair Emeritus of the communications department at Dominican University of California.

Ernest Green grew up attending church with his family and loved being a member of the Boy Scouts of America where he earned the rank of Eagle Scout. Ernest was the first black person to graduate from Central High School in Little Rock, Arkansas. His graduation was attended by the Reverend Martin Luther King, Jr. Ernest went on to attend Michigan State University, where he remained active in the civil rights movement. He graduated from Michigan State with a Bachelor of Arts, and later earned his Master of Sociology in 1964. He served as the Assistant Secretary of Labor from 1977 to 1981 under President Jimmy Carter.

Elizabeth Eckford left Central High School and moved to Ohio, where she finished high school and went on to attend Central State University, graduating with a bachelor's degree in History. She served in the United States Army for five years and now works as a probation officer in Little Rock. Elizabeth is the subject of a photograph that was the unanimous selection for the Pulitzer Prize in 1958 and that has come to epitomize the events of September 1957. In 2018, she published her autobiographical work, *The Worst First Day: Bullied While Desegregating Little Rock Central High.*

Minnijean Brown was expelled from Central High. While being harassed, she responded by calling a group of white students insulting names and dumping her lunch on them. After being expelled, Minnijean moved to New York. After finishing high school in New York, she attended college where she graduated with a bachelor's degree in Journalism. She is now a prominent political figure involved in civil rights issues.

Terrence Roberts moved to Los Angeles to finish high school and then attended California State University, where he graduated with a degree in sociology. He went on to receive a master's degree in social welfare from UCLA and a PhD in psychology at Southern Illinois University. He sat on several college and hospital boards before retiring to manage his consulting firm, Terrence Roberts Consulting. He published his memoirs, *Lessons from Little Rock*, in 2009 and a second book in 2010 called *Simple, Not Easy.*

Carlotta Walls graduated from Central High, despite being the subject of torment and harassment at the hands of students and staff. Carlotta's home was even bombed during the desegregation of Central High. She went on to graduate from Colorado State College and has spent the last thirty years working as a real estate broker. Carlotta has remained an activist and maintains memberships with the Colorado AIDS Project, Jack and Jill of America, the Urban League, and the NAACP.

Jefferson Thomas graduated from Central High in 1960 and went on to attend Los Angeles State College, where he earned a bachelor's degree in business administration and served as the president of the Associated Engineers. He went on to serve in the Vietnam War with the U.S. Army's 9th Infantry Division and later began a public speaking career on the topic of civil rights. Jefferson passed away due to pancreatic cancer in 2010.

Gloria Ray graduated from the Illinois Institute of Technology with a degree in Chemistry and Mathematics. She worked as a public school teacher for a few years before joining IBM's International Patent Operations in Sweden. She founded the international journal *Computers in Industry* and served as editor-in-chief in the early nineties, before going to work for Philips Telecommunications and Philips Lighting in the Netherlands. In 2019, she received an Honorary Doctorate of Science from the Illinois Institute of Technology for her outstanding contributions to the development of a more inclusive society. She currently resides in Sweden with her family.

Thelma Mothershed graduated from Central High School and went on to earn her bachelor's and master's degrees from Southern Illinois University. In 1958, she received the Spingarn Medal for outstanding achievement from the NAACP. She taught home economics in the St. Louis school system for 28 years before retiring in 1994. She has spent her life working to educate and protect women and those less fortunate. She has been given the Outstanding Role Model Award by the East St. Louis Chapter of the Top Ladies of Distinction. She was also presented with the National Humanitarian Award. In 2016, she received an Honorary Doctorate of Humane Letters from her alma mater, SIU.

George
MÜLLER

Guided by his faith, George Müller established 117 schools that taught more than 120,000 children. He also cared for over 10,000 orphans, making a significantly positive impact in the lives of countless people.

A Life of Dedication

Sometimes people make terrible choices. Sometimes, even if they are born to a loving mother and father, children choose to follow paths that take them away from the good things of the world and land them squarely in the midst of trouble, trouble, and more trouble.

In 1805, a boy named George was born in Kroppenstedt, Prussia, to a loving mother and father. Despite the good example set by his parents, he was drawn from a very young age to all the worst things that boys in those days could get themselves into.

If you were to follow young George as he snuck away from his house each morning, you would see him trampling the neighbor's rose bushes, charging after the fat tabby cat sunning herself peacefully on the porch, and picking the pockets of unsuspecting men as they opened carriage doors for young ladies—all before meeting up with his rugged and raucous friends for a day of drinking, smoking, and stealing.

You might see him spend the whole day gambling with money he had either stolen from strangers or cheated his friends out of. On especially bad days, you might see him take money from his hardworking father's wallet before he left the house—money he would use to pay off his gambling debts from the day before.

After watching George, it's entirely possible that you would decide that he wasn't a very good person. You might even think that he was pretty terrible. You would probably be shocked to learn that George was only ten years old—but it would be true.

By the time he was fourteen, he had become so hardened and immersed in riotous and wicked living that he didn't even bother to go home to see his sweet mother as she lay dying. He chose instead to spend the day drinking with his friends.

It would be easy to imagine that George was a lost cause and that someone so filled with love for the worst things life had to offer, who seemed to show so little care or compassion for others, would never amount to anything. But sometimes, just sometimes, people do change. Sometimes they awaken to their awful state and decide that they simply can't stand themselves for another moment and that something drastic must be done to turn things around.

And so it was for George.

Turning a Page

On a not-particularly-remarkable day in 1925, George was invited to a friend's house for a prayer meeting. He later recalled, "Despite my sinful lifestyle and cold heart, God had mercy on me. I was as careless as ever. I had no Bible and had not read any Scripture for years. I seldom went to church; and, out of custom only, I took the Lord's Supper twice a year. I never heard the gospel preached. Nobody told me that Jesus meant for Christians, by the help of God, to live according to the Holy Scriptures."

But something happened in George's heart in the cramped living room on that not-particularly-remarkable day. George would forever count that prayer meeting as the day that everything began to change. He said, "I have no doubt ... that He began a work of grace in me. Even though I scarcely had any knowledge of who God truly was, that evening was the turning point in my life."

George's father, thrilled at the change he saw in his son, hoped that he would continue on his newly righteous path and encouraged him to gain a religious education at the University of Halle. He secretly hoped that George would enter a life of service to God by becoming a clergyman, but he was happy just to see George interested in making something of himself.

While at Halle, George met a young woman who inspired him to continue making good choices and to keep drawing closer to God. He began studying scripture, praying regularly, and asking for forgiveness for what he now saw as the many sins he had committed against God and against his fellow man.

As George humbled himself, he felt the weight of his past mistakes being lifted from his shoulders. He felt alive, bright, and cheerful toward the whole world around him. He knew that even the most awful sinner could change his life and feel happy and hopeful, and he wanted to help other people feel as good as he did.

George had found his path.

He spent the next several years as a missionary, teaching the good things he had come to believe were true to anyone who seemed willing to hear his testimony. He worried about people who felt alone, sad, or hopeless—people like he had once been who didn't see any way out of lives that brought them little happiness or peace. He was especially concerned about children who didn't have loving adults to lead and guide them.

George Müller's Orphans

George married Mary Graves in the fall of 1830 and settled into life as a preacher in a small town in England. After just a few months, he became uncomfortable with the salary his position offered him; he feared that his congregation was paying tithes and offerings out of duty rather than because they wanted to, and he didn't think that was right. In fact, he didn't like a lot of the mixing of money and religion that he saw.

At that time, wealthy families were able to secure the best pews in the chapel by paying a fee to the church each month, but George didn't think that was right either. He felt that it gave the rich preferential access to the sermons being preached and didn't believe that money or status should have any place in the worship of God, so along with renouncing his salary, he also ended the practice of renting pews.

Mary agreed with George, and his faith that the Lord would provide for them and their needs without an official salary would become the pattern for the rest of their lives.

In 1834, George founded the Scriptural Knowledge Institution for Home and Abroad. Its purpose was to distribute Bibles and religious materials to anyone who wanted them and included the opening of day schools, Sunday schools, and adult schools that provided education founded on scriptural principles. Within its first year, there were five day schools—two for boys, and three for girls.

George and Mary continued to refuse a salary, or any kind of government assistance.

The children, many of whom had suffered very difficult and lonely lives, were overjoyed to be in the care of people as loving and kind as George and Mary. They sang songs as they did their chores, played games in the street, and chased chickens in the yard. There seemed to be an unending stream of giggling children, walking in groups of three or four between the four homes that comprised the Müller orphanage.

George and Mary's hearts burst with pride and gratitude as they watched all of their children grow and thrive.

But not everyone loved life on Wilson Street. By 1845, some neighbors became frustrated with the constant noise and commotion of 130 children running up and down the streets, singing and laughing at all hours of the day and night. They began to complain to George and Mary that something must be done to restore peace and serenity to the neighborhood.

Although George and Mary didn't see how the sounds of happy children could annoy, they also respected and loved their neighbors. They didn't want their good work to be a source of irritation for others, so they began making plans to build a new orphanage.

The Müllers had never received a regular wage, and they had refused every offer of government assistance. They had determined early on in life that if they were good stewards of all they had, then the Lord would always provide for their needs, and they didn't intend to start asking for money now. Things had always just seemed to work out for George and Mary, and they believed that they could continue to expect them to.

Blessings in Abundance

When they needed plans drawn up for the new orphanage, an accomplished architect approached them and asked if they would accept his work for free. He had heard of the good things they had done, and he wanted to lend his time and talents to help.

One day, after paying all of their bills for the month, George and Mary found themselves unable to put food on the breakfast table. There was simply no money left. Never one to doubt or worry, George sat the children down to the empty table and bowed his head in prayer. He asked for a blessing on the food they would eat, and gave thanks for all he had been blessed with.

Just then, a man knocked on the door. It was the town baker! He had brought a large basket full of fresh baked bread. Moments later, the milkman came to the door. His cart had broken down right in front of the orphanage and, rather than risk his milk spoiling in the sun as he repaired the cart, he gave it all to George and Mary and the children. Oh how sweet that breakfast tasted, as George and all of his children reflected on the goodness of their God and their neighbors.

Once, on a cold winter's night, the boilers in the home stopped working. The thought of his children shivering in unheated rooms caused George much heartache, but despite all of his efforts, the earliest any repairman would be able to come was the next morning. He and Mary tucked the children into bed with as many extra blankets as they could find and settled in for what they were sure would be a cold and difficult night. But something strange happened. As the children drifted off to sleep, the cold wind died down, the temperature outside rose, and a warm wind began to blow. It blew through the cracks in the windows and up through the floorboards, and the children slept peacefully—warm and cozy—all through the night. After the boiler repairman left the next morning, the cold and bitter wind returned.

In all, it cost the Müllers the equivalent of millions of dollars in today's terms in order to furnish their five homes, but they never asked anyone for donations, and they never went into debt. By 1949, the new orphanage was complete, and 300 more children entered into the watchful care of George and Mary Müller. George was always careful to give thanks for what he had and to credit the generosity of strangers and the answers to prayers for his ability to feed, house, and educate his many charges. He noted that he always wrote down his prayers, so that when, in His own time, the Lord answered them, he could be sure to record it as a blessing. His journals and autobiography are full of prayers and answers to prayers, with entries like this:

> "A brother in the Lord came to me this morning and, after a few minutes of conversation gave me two thousand pounds for furnishing the new Orphan House ... Now I am able to meet all of the expenses. In all probability I will even have several hundred pounds more than I need. The Lord not only gives as much

as is absolutely necessary for his work, but he gives abundantly. This blessing filled me with inexplicable delight. He had given me the full answer to my thousands of prayers during the [past] 1,195 days."

The blessings would continue to come, and George and Mary would continue to teach and house their orphans. George was a meticulous recordkeeper and budgeter, and the history of every donation ever given to his charity, along with every expense, is recorded in his autobiographical work. He wanted everyone who showed him generosity to know that their gift was being put to good and honest use.

Their work continued until 1870, when Mary died. At the time of her death, the Müllers had 1,720 children in their care and had sent countless more out into the world—armed with love-filled childhoods, life and spiritual knowledge, and apprenticeships, professional training, or jobs. George made sure that each child who left the orphanage left with the skills they would need for a prosperous and successful life. They were also each given a Bible and a trunk with two nice changes of clothes. And of course, they always knew that the doors to "home" and the loving embraces of Mary and George would be there whenever they needed them.

After Mary's death, George remarried and embarked on a new mission. At the age of seventy, he and his wife, Susannah, set out on what would become a seventeen-year mission trip. They taught the gospel in countries such as England, Scotland, Ireland, Switzerland, The Netherlands, Canada, France, Spain, Italy, Egypt, Palestine, Syria, Turkey, Greece, Hungary, Russia, Poland, India, Australia,

China, Japan, Singapore, New Zealand, Tasmania, and many others. In total, they visited and taught in more than 34 countries and traveled over 200,000 miles.

They never received a regular wage, they never took money from the government, and they never asked anyone to donate to their work.

George Müller died at the age of 87. He spent his life in selfless service to those who couldn't advocate for or help themselves. He protected the weak and innocent, and he gave hope to thousands who were otherwise hopeless. His life reminds us that we can always change, that it is never too late to be more than we were before, and that it is always worth our time and effort to show love and compassion to those who are suffering or in need.

As a young man, George would have been content to spend his life gambling, drinking, and stealing. But sometimes the universe has other plans for us, and we have to get down to the business of making ourselves into better people, so that we can do the important things we were meant to do. It's always worth the work it takes to be better than we used to be.

Edward
SNOWDEN

Choosing to break the law in order to do what he thought was right, Edward Snowden publicly shared a significant number of secret documents that exposed the government's widespread surveillance of innocent people all over the world.

Gamer, Geek, Traitor, Patriot

Lindsay Mills arrived at Oahu's airport an hour early. Even though she and Ed had been together for eight years, she still cared about making a good impression on his mom. In spite of the fact that she was currently furious with Ed, Lindsay was determined to give his mother, Wendy, a proper "aloha" welcome and had stopped to pick up a lei. Its sweet smell wafted out of the plastic box and filled her car.

How could he just up and disappear?! He was the one who had been so insistent that his mother take leave from her job with the district court of Baltimore and come to Honolulu for a visit. He'd planned the whole trip! And now, the day his mom was arriving, he'd just taken off on one of his stupid last-minute "business" trips. And yet, even as she fumed, she reasoned with herself that it really wasn't right of her to be mad. She knew the nature of his work, and she had long ago accepted that sometimes he would have to go away on trips at the last minute, and that sometimes he wouldn't even be able to tell her where he was going or how long he'd be gone.

But still... something felt off. She just couldn't shake the feeling that something was wrong. She couldn't believe that he'd miss his mom's visit. It just wasn't like Ed.

Turning her attention back to Wendy, she parked the car and went into the airport to wait, the plastic box with the sweet-smelling lei tucked under her arm. Ed's mom loved her boy and always looked forward to her time with him. Lindsay felt bad for her—in a minute, she'd get off the plane, excited to see her son, and then she'd have to politely hide her disappointment when she realized Lindsay was alone.

The whole thing was just crummy.

Vanished Without a Trace

The next night at dinner, Lindsay did her best to be a happy hostess. She and Wendy made small talk and finalized some plans for the week they'd spend together. They'd known each other for a long time and had a good relationship. Lindsay was looking forward to exploring the island with someone new, and she was especially excited to catch an island hopper over to the Big Island to visit Kilauea. She and Ed always talked about checking out the volcano, but the last year had been kind of rough, and they hadn't been able to get out as much as they used to.

Wendy kept talking about Ed's health. She just couldn't understand why he was gone. Wasn't he supposed to be on medical leave? How could they call him away for a work trip when he was on medical leave? What if he'd had one of his seizures? What if something was wrong and he was alone and needed help? Lindsay kept trying to assure her that it was normal for Ed to get called away, but the more she said it, the more she had to acknowledge that it wasn't normal at all. Sure, when they'd lived in Japan it was normal. When he'd lived in Switzerland it was normal. But since they'd been in Hawaii with his new job, he hadn't been called away one single time.

Lindsay looked across the table with tears in her eyes. When Wendy saw them, her eyes welled too. They held hands as the tears fell. Something was wrong, and the two women who loved Edward Snowden the most in the world knew it.

A Tradition of Service

Edward Joseph Snowden was born June 21, 1983, in Elizabeth City, North Carolina. His family had been in North Carolina since before the Revolutionary War and had been Americans for about as long as it was possible for someone to be an American. His earliest American ancestor was immortalized in a poem by Henry Wadsworth Longfellow (whom he also happened to be related to) titled, *The Courtship of Miles Standish*, which describes the love the commander of the Plymouth colony had for one Miss Priscilla Mullins:

> Nothing was heard in the room but the hurrying pen of the Stripling,
>
> Busily writing epistles important, to go by the Mayflower,
>
> Ready to sail on the morrow, or next day at latest, God Willing!
>
> Homeward bound with the tidings of all that terrible winter,
>
> Letters written by Alden, and full of the name of Priscilla,
>
> Full of the name and the fame of the Puritan maiden Priscilla!

Alas, for all his pining, Miles would not win the heart of the fair Priscilla, who would instead marry another passenger on the *Mayflower*, John Alden. It was through their lineage that Edward would eventually come into the world.

In his book, *Permanent Record*, Snowden described his American ancestry like this:

> My mother's side fought in every war in my country's history, from the Revolution and the Civil War (in which the Carolinian relatives fought for the Confederacy against their New England/Union cousins), to both world wars. Mine is a family that has always answered the call of duty.

Edward was always proud of his American heritage and of the members of his family who served with distinction in defense of his country. Even those who didn't serve in the military still served in other federal positions, and he always knew he would follow in their footsteps. Snowdens worked for the US government—that's just the way it was, and the way it had always been.

Ed spent most of his youth and childhood playing video games and learning to code. Computers just "clicked" for him, and his parents often worried that he spent too much time in front of a screen and too little time outside doing kid things with his peers. Sometimes he tried to pacify his parents by doing "normal" things, but the only place he really felt like himself was in the digital world he had created.

When other teenagers were playing sports and hanging out at the mall trying to impress girls, he was in chat rooms learning how to hack. He didn't speak the language of other kids his age, but he spoke "geek" fluently—this world made sense to him. He hated school and wasn't too upset when a bad bout with mononucleosis caused him to miss a whole nine months of his freshman year of high school.

Instead of going back, he talked his parents into letting him take the GED, which he easily passed. He was free.

He spent the next few years drifting in and out of college classes, which he rarely finished, and putting his computer skills to work as a freelancer. He earned decent money and felt like he was in a good place. Until one September morning, when everything changed.

9/11

All of Ed's family lived or worked in Washington, DC, or New York. His grandfather had retired from the Coast Guard and now worked as a senior official in the FBI, spending a lot of time at the Pentagon. His grandmother spent a lot of time in New York.

When the planes hit the first and then the second towers of the World Trade Center, Edward (and the rest of the world) knew that this was no accident. He was working at Fort Meade when the news reports of a third plane hitting the Pentagon began to fill the airwaves. Word spread quickly that the base was going to be locked down, and he was caught in the flood of cars trying to get out of there before it was too late.

As he drove, his fingers fumbled on the buttons of his cell phone. It seemed like everyone in the country was making calls at the same time, and he got busy signal after busy signal. Finally, he heard his mom's voice. She didn't know where anyone was—Gran could be in New York today, Pops might be at the Pentagon. She couldn't remember, and she couldn't get a hold of anyone. No one knew exactly what was going on, but everyone knew one thing: American was under attack.

Each generation has an event that shapes their recollection of time. For Ed's great-grandparents, it was the Great Depression; for his Gran and Pops, it was the attack on Pearl Harbor; his parents remembered the Vietnam War; and although he didn't know it yet, Ed's generation would divide time into the years before, and those after, September 11th, 2001.

He would later write,

> Nearly three thousand people died on 9/11. Imagine everyone you love, everyone you know, even everyone with a familiar name or just a familiar face—and image they're gone. Imagine the empty houses. Imagine the empty school, the empty classrooms. All those people you lived among and who together formed the fabric of your days, just not there anymore. The events of 9/11 left holes. Holes in families, holes in communities. Holes in the ground.

> Now, consider this: over one million people have been killed in the course of America's response.

> The two decades since 9/11 have been a litany of American destruction by way of American self-destruction, with the promulgation of secret policies, secret laws, secret courts, and secret wars, whose traumatizing impact—whose very existence—the US government has repeatedly classified, denied, disclaimed, and distorted. After having spent roughly half that period as an employee of the American

Intelligence Community and roughly the other half in exile, I know better than most how often the agencies get things wrong. I know, too, how the collection and analysis of intelligence can inform the production of disinformation and propaganda, for use as frequently against America's allies as its enemies—and sometimes against its own citizens. Yet even given that knowledge, I still struggle to accept the sheer magnitude and speed of the change, from an America that sought to define itself by a calculated and performative respect for dissent to a security state whose militarized police demand obedience, drawing their guns and issuing the order for total submission now heard in every city: "Stop resisting."

This is why whenever I try to understand how the last two decades happened, I return to that September—to that ground-zero day and its immediate aftermath. To return to that fall means coming up against a truth darker than the lies that tied the Taliban to al-Qaeda and conjured up Saddam Hussein's illusory stockpile of WMDs. It means, ultimately, confronting the fact that the carnage and abuses that marked my young adulthood were born not only in the executive branch and the intelligence agencies, but also in the hearts and minds of all Americans, myself included.

Of course, the Ed of September 11th, 2001, couldn't know all that the Ed of today knows, and so, with the patriotism of his ancestors coursing through his veins, he abandoned his childish pursuits and signed up to serve his country in whatever capacity she had need of him.

A Terrible Discovery

Ed enlisted in the Army, where he became a Special Forces candidate. Injuries during his training would leave him ineligible for service, but his sharp mind and knack for computers caught the attention of the intelligence community. By 2005, he was working for the Central Intelligence Agency, where he spent the next four years. While there, he witnessed things that made him question the integrity and tactics of his employer (the US government). He tried to raise his concerns to his superiors, but they just laughed him off. In 2009, he resigned from the CIA and took a position with the National Security Agency.

A pattern began where Ed would progress in his job, gaining more responsibility and, with it, more access to the inner workings of the agency that employed him. Each time he was given access to more information, he found more things to be concerned about. One such source of concern was when he discovered that the government had created a secret system that allowed them to collect personal information about every single person in the United States.

At first, he only knew about this domestic spying because of his access to the deepest workings of the CIA, but later, he would see it firsthand. He worked in a building where young intelligence officers routinely looked through personal and private photos that young women and men had on their phones. Private pictures, phone calls, text messages, and emails were collected, looked at, and stored in massive data-collection centers. The government said that they needed to collect this information because of what had happened on September 11th. They argued that the only way to keep Americans safe was to know what everyone was doing at all times—but promised that they would never use it unless they absolutely had to.

Ed remembered September 11th, but he didn't think that what the government was doing was right, and he didn't see how it was keeping Americans safe.

The United States of America was spying on its own citizens. Conversations between husbands and wives, correspondence between doctors and patients—everything was being collected. And much of it was being looked at by Ed's coworkers—not for national security reasons, but because they were nosy and bored.

In 2013, Verizon Wireless came under scrutiny when it was revealed that they were turning over customer information to the NSA. Congress launched an investigation to determine if anything illegal had been done or if Verizon had broken any laws. Ed knew that the NSA had been spying on Americans for years, and he hoped that this investigation would set things right. He hoped that the government for which his family had worked and fought for two hundred years would root out the corruption that he knew had taken over the intelligence community and restore the United States to its former greatness.

Ed watched on March 15, 2013, as James Clapper, the Director of National Intelligence, testified before Congress. His heart and hope for his country sank as he heard Clapper lie under oath.

"Does the NSA collect any type of data at all on millions or hundreds of millions of Americans?" Senator Ron Wyden asked Clapper.

"No, sir," Clapper replied.

Edward knew what he had to do.

Whistleblower

A week had passed, and still no word from Ed.

Lindsay dropped Wendy off at the Honolulu airport, and they promised each other they'd call if they heard any news. They hugged each other tight—neither of them wanted to let go. Lindsay drove home in a daze. What on earth was going on? Where was Ed? She couldn't believe he'd completely missed his mom's visit.

When she got home, she flopped into the chair at Ed's desk. It smelled like him, and she started to feel worried again. She wiggled the mouse, and the monitor sprang to life. Something caught her eye. Ed's Skype status had changed.

"Sorry but it had to be done," it read.

Lindsay's heart sank, and her palms began to sweat. What did it mean? What had to be done? Where was Ed, and why was he sorry? And why had he chosen such a strange way to apologize?

In the weeks that followed, Lindsay would learn along with the rest of the world what Ed's cryptic message meant.

First from Hong Kong, and later from Russia, Edward Snowden would tell Americans what their government was doing. Lindsay watched his first video from her friend's living room floor.

I calmly waited for the 12-minute YouTube video to load. And then there he was. Real. Alive. I was shocked. He looked thin, but he sounded like his old self. The old Ed, confident and strong. Like how he was before this last tough year. This was the man I loved, not the cold distant ghost I'd recently been living with. I didn't know what to say. Ed, what have you done? How can you come back from this?

Lindsay would continue to learn about Ed's revelations along with the rest of the world. There was no communication from him—she realized finally what he had done. She saw the care he had taken to protect her and his family from what he was about to do. He had insisted that his mother come visit because he didn't want her or Lindsay to be alone when the news broke. He wanted them to have each other for support.

As the FBI began their investigation, Lindsay wasn't forced to choose between telling the truth and protecting the man she loved—Ed had ensured that she could answer every question in her weeks of interrogation honestly. She truly knew nothing. Ed had kept all blame and all responsibility for his actions squarely on himself.

In her journal, Lindsay wrote about her first call with Wendy after they learned what Ed had done:

> Had a phone call with Wendy, where we both said that however badly Ed hurt us, he did the right thing by trying to ensure that when he was gone, Wendy and I were together. That's why he'd invited her and been so insistent about her coming. He'd wanted us to be together in Hawaii when he went public so that we could

keep each other company and give each other strength and comfort. It's so hard to be angry at someone you love. And even harder to be angry at someone you love and respect for doing the right thing.

Exile

The US government charged Edward Snowden with espionage and theft of government property. He had stolen a million documents that proved the illegal activity of those within the intelligence community, and he had handed over tens of thousands of them to journalists, who were carefully searching them for information that the American people deserved to know. His passport was revoked, and he was labeled an international fugitive. No country wanted to give him refuge, and the US desperately wanted him back.

Snowden was eventually granted asylum in Russia, where he has been for the last seven years. All of the documents he had that proved that the government was spying on Americans were handed over to American journalists or destroyed before he traveled to Russia. He was afraid that Russia might want to use him to get classified information on the United States, and he was unwilling to be a party to betraying his country to another.

Lindsay eventually flew to Russia to join Ed, and the two were married at a Moscow courthouse in 2017. Because the US government still wants to arrest Ed for telling the world that they were spying on their own citizens, the Snowdens have to be very careful about where they go and what they do. They are together, and they are safe, but they are not free. They sacrificed their futures and their freedom so that their fellow Americans would know that their rights were being infringed on by their government.

Viewing the destruction of their lives, Lindsay wrote,

> I remember the trip Wendy and I took to Kilauea. The guide said that volcanoes are only destructive in the short term. In the long term, they move the world. They create islands, cool the planet, and enrich the soil. Their lava flows uncontrolled and then cools and hardens. The ash they shoot into the air sprinkles down as minerals, which fertilize the earth and make new life grow.

Sometimes, great disruptions and short-term destructions are necessary in order for new life to grow and old things to be cleaned away. And sometimes, if we are lucky, there are people like Ed Snowden who are willing to sacrifice for a greater good, asking only that their sacrifice not be made in vain. Ed gave his countrymen the information they needed to hold their government accountable for the wrong things it was doing. He left it up to them to do the rest.

Frederick
DOUGLASS

After escaping from slavery, Frederick became a national leader of the abolition effort, praised for his sharp abilities in speaking and writing to attack the evils of slavery and the need for social reform.

Speaking for Truth

Frederick Douglass stood at the podium, gripping it with trembling, clammy hands. Before him sat abolitionists who had come from near and far to the Massachusetts island of Nantucket to hear him speak. At only twenty-three years of age, Frederick had never spoken before so many people. He thought he might be sick.

As his stomach heaved and the sweat beaded on his brow, he reminded himself how important this was—how the world needed to hear the things he had to say—and his heart began to take up a more steady rhythm. This wasn't about him. This was about something much bigger than one man. He opened his mouth, and began to speak, the words coming softly at first, but then building in volume and force until his audience sat wide-eyed and captivated by his first-hand account of life as a slave.

Born the son of an enslaved woman and fathered by an unknown white man, Frederick Augustus Washington Bailey was born early in 1818 on the eastern shores of Maryland. Frederick spent the majority of his early years with his grandparents and an aunt. He would only see his mother a handful of times before her death when he was only seven years old.

During his early childhood, Frederick was exposed to the atrocities and humiliation of slavery, where he would witness firsthand brutal whippings and abuse. He spent many a long night cold and without food. When Frederick was only eight, he was sent away from his family to Baltimore to live with a ship carpenter named Hugh Auld. Hugh's wife took a liking to young Frederick and made sure that he was always well fed and that he always had clothes that fit and enough blankets at night. She thought it would be good for him to learn to read and even began teaching Frederick the alphabet.

One day, Hugh walked in on his wife teaching Frederick. He became angry and explained to her that teaching a slave to read would only end up hurting him in the long run. He said that the more slaves were able to learn about the world and the institution of slavery, the more they would realize how hopeless their situation was. He argued that it was better for everyone for slaves to remain illiterate and ignorant and that they would be happier in the long run that way.

But Frederick understood what Hugh was saying, and it made him even more determined to learn to read. He began rushing through his work, finishing as quickly as he could, so that he would have a few moments to spare before moving on to the next task. In these stolen moments, he would sneak into the library and practice his reading on any printed thing he could get close to. Convinced by her husband's arguments, Mrs. Auld began hiding her books from Frederick, even taking care to keep the Bible out of his sight.

But Frederick wouldn't be deterred. He was determined to learn to read and write, and no measures would be enough to keep him in ignorance. He began saving portions of his meals to take to town and trade with the poor and hungry white children in town. Frederick was wel -fed with the Aulds as his masters, and food was always set out for him to snack on whenever he was hungry. In contrast, many poor white families didn't have enough to eat, but their children were taught to read in school. Frederick saw that he and his young friends were both hungering for different things: Frederick was hungry for knowledge that he couldn't gain on his own, and his friends in town were plagued with hungry bellies. The boys realized that they could help feed each other the things they most craved.

And so it was that the slave boy, Frederick, learned to read and write.

It was in Baltimore that Frederick first heard the word "abolition" and realized that there were white people in the North who didn't own slaves and wanted to help slaves gain their freedom. He also learned for the first time that there were free blacks living and working in other parts of the country. A new world was opening up to Frederick's mind. "Going to live at Baltimore," Frederick said, "laid the foundation, and opened the gateway to all my subsequent prosperity."

"The more I read, the more I was led to abhor and detest my enslavers. I could regard them in no other light than a band of successful robbers, who had left their homes, and gone to Africa, and stolen us from our homes, and in a strange land reduced us to slavery. I loathed them as being the meanest as well as the most wicked of men. As I read and contemplated the subject, behold! that very discontentment which Master Hugh had predicted would follow my learning to read had already come, to torment and sting my soul to unutterable anguish. As I writhed under it, I would at times feel that learning to read had been a curse rather than a blessing. It had given me a view of my wretched condition, without the remedy. It opened my eyes to the horrible pit, but to no ladder upon which to get out. In moments of agony, I envied my fellow-slaves for their stupidity. I have often wished myself a beast. I preferred the condition of the meanest reptile to my own. Any thing, no matter what, to get rid of thinking! It was this everlasting thinking of my condition that tormented me. There was no getting rid of it. It was pressed upon me by every object within sight or hearing, animate or inanimate. The silver trump of freedom had roused my soul to eternal wakefulness. Freedom now appeared, to disappear no more forever. It was heard in every sound and seen in every thing. It was ever present to torment me with a sense of my wretched condition. I saw nothing without seeing it, I heard nothing without hearing it, and felt nothing without feeling it. It looked from every star, it smiled in every calm, breathed in every wind, and moved in every storm."

Frederick would spend seven seemingly decent and almost comfortable years in Baltimore before being sent back to his owner, Hugh's brother, Thomas Auld. He lived for a brief time with Thomas before being rented out to a poor farmer named Edward Covey. Edward was a brutish man who had the reputation of being a "slave breaker."

In Covey's possession, Frederick was beaten nearly daily. So bad were his whippings that the stripes on his back rarely had time to begin to heal before they were torn open again. Food was withheld from him, and his body was exposed to the harsh elements. Covey believed that slaves were more obedient and useful when they were beaten and humiliated into submission, and this was what he attempted to do to Frederick. When recounting his first few months with Covey, Frederick would remark that he had set out to "break me in body, soul, and spirit," and that he had succeeded.

Then one day, when Frederick was sixteen, he determined that he would not submit to another brutal lashing. This day, when Edward Covey raised the whip, Frederick turned on him, grabbing him and wrestling the savage tool from his hands and forcing Covey to the ground. His fight with Covey was recounted in his book, *Narrative of the Life of Frederick Douglass, an American Slave*, in which he said, "You have seen how a man was made a slave; you shall see how a slave was made a man." Covey never laid a hand on Frederick again, and something changed in Frederick's mind. He had learned something valuable about the nature of man; never again would he cower in fear of another person.

> "If there is no struggle, there is no progress. Those who profess to favor freedom, and yet depreciate agitation, are men who want crops without plowing up the ground. They want rain without thunder and lightning. They want the ocean without the awful roar of its many waters. This struggle may be a moral one; or it may be a physical one; or it may be both moral and physical; but it must be a struggle. Power concedes nothing without a demand. It never did and it never will."

A Slave No More

Frederick knew that he could no longer live as a slave. He

made plans to escape within the year, but on the morning he had selected, his plans were ruined and his hopes of escape dashed. He would have to wait two more years before the opportunity for escape presented itself again. This time, he resolved, he would gain his freedom or die trying!

Frederick had met a free woman named Anna, and the two fell in love and decided to marry. Anna helped Frederick plan his escape from Baltimore by getting him a Naval uniform and, with the help of friends, securing travel papers and a false identity. On the morning of September 3, 1838, Frederick boarded a train in Baltimore. He then took a steamboat, followed by another train, and in less than 24 hours, Frederick had left his old life and the chains of slavery behind forever. He arrived in New York City where Anna joined him, and the two were married. A month later, they traveled to New Bedford, Massachusetts, where he changed his name to Frederick Douglass, and set about building a life as a free man.

Forever diligent and striving to better himself, Douglass would continue to hone his reading and writing skills for the rest of his life. He joined numerous social groups in New Bedford, including a black Christian church attended by Harriet Tubman and Sojourner Truth. Frederick frequently would attend meetings for abolitionists where he found comfort and inspiration in minds and hearts that worked like his. He went to listen to William Lloyd Garrison speak at an anti-slavery rally and later wrote, "No face and form ever impressed me with such sentiments [the hatred of slavery] as did those of William Lloyd Garrison." Garrison was a white abolitionist who believed that the Constitution of the United States was a pro-slavery document and that the union should be destroyed in order to abolish slavery. Although Frederick at first agreed, he was later influenced by Lysander Spooner's writings on the Constitution that argued that it could actually be a force for good against slavery and that it was a document that favored abolition.

Although Garrison and Douglass would be close friends and allies for many years—it was Garrison who arranged for Douglass to give his first public speech in Nantucket—they would eventually part ways as their visions for abolition and the future of the United States took drastically different paths.

A Way with Words

Those who stood in the crowd and listened to a nervous, 23-year-old Douglass recount his life's experiences would be forever moved. One reporter wrote, "Flinty hearts were pierced, and cold ones melted by his eloquence."

Douglass's eloquence and talent as an orator would impress audiences throughout his life. His ability to weave touching stories and condemning sermons with expert use of the English language flew in the face of the pro-slavery narrative that black people were unequal to whites in intelligence and ability and that they wouldn't be able to live as free people amongst the white population of the United States. Northerners, by contrast, couldn't believe that the man they saw before them in his sharp black suit and tie, who spoke with more skillful prose than most whites, had ever been the property of another man—beaten and whipped and forced to labor in fields.

Despite an uneasy feeling that publishing his story might endanger his freedom, Douglass published his autobiography, *Narrative of the Life of Frederick Douglass, an American Slave*. The year was 1845, and the book quickly became a bestseller. Three years later, after a public speaking tour that took him all over England, Ireland, and Scotland, Douglass published the first issue of his newest project, the *North Star*, a four-page weekly newspaper. In it, he took to task the hypocrisy he saw within the Christian community in the United States, saying,

> "I therefore hate the corrupt, slaveholding, women-whipping, cradle-plundering, partial and hypocritical Christianity of the land... I look upon it as the climax of all misnomers, the boldest of all frauds, and the grossest of all libels. Never was there a clearer case of 'stealing the livery of the court of heaven to serve the devil in.' I am filled with unutterable loathing when I contemplate the religious pomp and show, together with the horrible inconsistencies, which every where surround me. We have men-stealers for ministers, women-whippers for missionaries, and cradle-plunderers for church members. The man who wields the blood-clotted cowskin during the week fills the pulpit on Sunday, and claims to be a minister of the meek and lowly Jesus. . . . The slave auctioneer's bell and the church-going bell chime in with each other, and the bitter cries of the heart-broken slave are drowned in the religious shouts of his pious master. Revivals of religion and revivals in the slave-trade go hand in hand together. The slave prison and the church stand near each other. The clanking of fetters and the rattling of chains in the prison, and the pious

psalm and solemn prayer in the church, may be heard at the same time. The dealers in the bodies of men erect their stand in the presence of the pulpit, and they mutually help each other. The dealer gives his blood-stained gold to support the pulpit, and the pulpit, in return, covers his infernal business with the garb of Christianity. Here we have religion and robbery the allies of each other—devils dressed in angels' robes, and hell presenting the semblance of paradise."

A Love of All Mankind

Although Douglass would speak harshly about slavery and slave-holders in general his entire life, he believed that it was his duty to treat all men as equals and that the Lord required that he love all men as well. Despite having every reason to hate those who had caused him so much harm, he endeavored instead to educate them in the wrongness of their thinking and the consequences of their actions. In 1855, he wrote an open letter to his old master, Thomas Auld, from whom supporters had purchased his freedom several years earlier. In it, he laid open for all to see the atrocities committed by his master against him and other slaves and compared it to the generally accepted treatment of all slaves by all slaveholders.

In one particularly poignant paragraph, he asks Auld to imagine what he would feel if his own children were handled in the same manner he handled the children of slaves. He said,

> How, let me ask, would you look upon me, were I, some dark night, in company with a band of hardened

villains, to enter the precincts of your elegant dwelling, and seize the person of your own lovely daughter, Amanda, and carry her off from your family, friends, and all the loved ones of her youth—make her my slave—compel her to work, and I take her wages— place her name on my ledger as property—disregard her personal rights—fetter the powers of her immortal soul by denying her the right and privilege of learning to read and write—feed her coarsely—clothe her scantily, and whip her on the naked back occasionally; more, and still more horrible, leave her unprotected—a degraded victim to the brutal lust of fiendish overseers, who would pollute, blight, and blast her fair soul—rob her of all dignity—destroy her virtue, and annihilate in her person all the graces that adorn the character of virtuous womanhood? I ask, how would you regard me, if such were my conduct? Oh! the vocabulary of the damned would not afford a word sufficiently infernal to express your idea of my God-provoking wickedness. Yet, sir, your treatment of my beloved sisters is in all essential points precisely like the case I have now supposed. Damning as would be such a deed on my part, it would be no more so than that which you have committed against me and my sisters.

His letter was read by the very girl he asked his old master to imagine being kidnapped and ill-used. Amanda Auld sought out Frederick and traveled north to hear one of his speeches. She cheered from the crowd and later met him and offered her apologies for the way her father had treated him and his other slaves. Thomas, it is said, applauded his daughter's actions.

Many years later, as Auld lay dying in his bed, Frederick Douglass would go to his old master. He sat with him, and the two men reconciled their past. Frederick forgave the man who had abused and mishandled him as a piece of property rather than treating him as a human being, and gave him the gift of death with a clean conscience, leaving him to sort out the rewards for his actions with his Maker.

Douglass would speak and write for causes of freedom and human dignity for the rest of his life. He lent his skills as speaker and writer to the cause of women's suffrage, becoming an outspoken advocate for the rights of women to vote. He advised President Lincoln and, later, Presidents Johnson and Grant on race relations and the plight of blacks in America. He authored books, published essays, and preached sermons from pulpits in black and white churches alike. He held government positions and was visited and consulted by heads of state. He helped slaves escape along the Underground Railroad and helped the country heal after the end of the Civil War.

He died in Washington, D.C., at the age of 77. His love for mankind, be they black or white, bond or free, male or female, typified his life. His work was often with causes and people prone to contention. He refused to let politics or alliances get in the way of what he saw as the more important work and was known to break with friends and partner with others who might have been viewed as enemies, if it meant that he would be able to bring about the changes he felt were important, saying, "I would unite with anybody to do right and with nobody to do wrong."

His moral character, like his speech and mastery of the written word, was impeccable.

Mercy Otis
WARREN

Sometimes writing under a pen name,
Mercy Otis Warren was a persuasive
writer whose political poems and
pamphlets inspired support for
independence from the British empire.

The Power of Words

Mercy Otis was born in the year 1728 to a well known and wealthy family in Cape Cod, Massachusetts. She was the third of thirteen children. Growing up, Mercy received an unusual education. You see, she was born into a family that believed that law, literature, and politics were of utmost importance, and so around dinner tables and over cups of tea, her father—a successful attorney and politician—led the family in rousing debates and stories of political theatrics and the rights and duties of the people.

It wasn't common for girls to be formally educated in Mercy's time, but her family always encouraged her to seek new knowledge and to not pay any mind to what others felt women should or shouldn't learn. Although not *technically* permitted to join, Mercy was able to listen in on lessons by standing just outside the door of the classroom where her uncle, Reverend Jonathan Russell, taught her brothers. Eventually, Rev. Russell invited her into the classroom, and Mercy began to participate and learn alongside her brothers in nearly every subject.

From the time she was very young, Mercy loved to read. She would often sneak into her uncle's library to scour his massive book collection for works that piqued her interest. These excursions into worlds unknown through the pages of the best books of the time ignited in Mercy a love of poetry, drama, and political activism.

Mercy the Activist

As Mercy grew into adulthood she learned from her brother, an outspoken political activist named James Otis, who had a hand in many of the events that would lead up to the American Revolution. James coined the phrase, "Taxation without representation is tyranny." He authored many important pamphlets and used his position as a lawyer to fight injustice. He believed that "The colonists are by the law of nature freeborn, as indeed all men are, white or black."

James heavily influenced Mercy, and she loved and admired him.

When Mercy was twenty-six years old she married James Warren, a merchant who served in the state legislature. James admired Mercy and thought she had a brilliant mind and a talent for words. He always encouraged Mercy to pursue her writing. They had five children together, but despite the demands of motherhood and the responsibility of women in those days to run and manage a household, Mercy was still drawn to politics, and before long she was swept up amongst revolutionary thinkers and anti-federalists. Between her brother's involvement in politics and her husband's involvement in government, Mercy found herself in the midst of the men and events that would shape the colonies' relationship with Great Britain and eventually lead to a full-fledged revolution.

When Mercy was forty-one, her beloved brother was savagely assaulted by colonial officers. The head injury he suffered left him forever altered, and he faded from the public eye. He was no longer able to practice law, and he stopped speaking publicly. Mary had had enough. Despite being involved by association throughout the majority of her adulthood, Mercy dedicated herself to a life of political activism. She often held protest gatherings in her home, and these protests soon became the Committees of Correspondence.

With a fiery belief system and a unique point of view, Mercy Otis Warren began writing poems and articles that were published in Boston newspapers. She called the people to action. She demanded they stand up to the unjust rule of King George, and she inspired them through her wit and passion to take a side in the cause of freedom.

Mercy the Wordsmith

Mercy's words had power. Consider this example:

> "America stands armed with resolution and virtue. But she still recoils at the idea of drawing the sword against the nation from whence she derived her origin. Yet Britain, like an unnatural parent, is ready to plunge her dagger into the bosom of her affectionate offspring. But may we not hope for more lenient measures."

Mercy started crafting political dramas that rejected British policies and mocked well-known officials in her state, most notably Massachusetts governor Thomas Hutchinson. She published her satirical piece titled "The Adulator" (or "The Puppet") because she knew that many people didn't want to listen to what women had to say about politics. She didn't care, so long as her messages were being heard loud and clear. And they were!

In "The Adulator" Mercy denounced the British colonial governor's policies and called out those who were in power. She was a revolutionary of the revolution—writing pieces that critiqued pre-Revolutionary War America a full four years before The Declaration of Independence was written. Mercy was a radical supporter of the Boston Tea Party boycotts and used her influence to call for boycotts of all other imports from The Crown. She encouraged her fellow women to follow in her footsteps. She made rebellion patriotic! And the people followed her calls—inspired by her passion and her courageous words.

In the early days of the American Revolution, Mercy began to write about what she thought and witnessed. She filled pages with ideas and firsthand accounts of the things she was experiencing as a woman on the forefront of the movement. This text was published in 1805 and titled, *History of the Rise, Progress and Termination of the American Revolution*. It was one of the first nonfiction books to ever be published in the United States by a woman. Mercy believed strongly in the preservation of human rights, which were at the forefront of the anti-federalist cause, and she hoped that her outspoken words and ideas would lead to liberty-protecting policies in the new United States that would endure forever.

Mercy applauded radical revolutionaries like Samuel Adams, Patrick Henry, and Thomas Jefferson—great men who are often referred to as the Founding Fathers of America. She was known to be disapproving of those she believed worked against the revolution or made it more difficult. She had become acquainted and friendly with John Adams and his wife, Abigail, who traveled in the same revolutionary circles as Mercy and John Warren, often corresponding with them. At one point, John Adams called Mercy "the most accomplished woman in America."

Yet even he was not always safe from Mercy's pen. After Mercy wrote of her frustration with John Adams, he sent her a letter addressing the issue and defending himself:

July 20th 1807

Dear Madam,

In the 392 Page of the third Volume of your History you say that "After Mr Adams's return from England, he was implicated, by a large portion of his Countrymen, as having relinquished the Republican System, And forgotten the Principles of the American Revolution, which he had advocated for near twenty years."

I am somewhat at a loss for the meaning of the Word implicated in this place. If it means Suspected, or accused, or reproached, I know nothing of it. No Man ever accused or reproached me, with any such Relinquishment or Oblivion. My Books had been received and read. The first Volume had been published in three new Editions of it, one in Boston, another at Nᴇw York, and a third at Philadelphia and propagated far and wide in all parts of the United States. It was put into the hands of the Members of the Continental Convention at Philadelphia then sitting for the formation of the Constitution in 1787, and almost in despair of ever agreeing upon any Plan. This Book had such an Effect upon the Gentlemen that it united them in the System they adopted.

Your Friend Mr Dickenson came out of the Convention and said to Dr Rush, that he had been in despair of getting the Convention to agree at all. But

Mr Adams's Book had diffused among the Members such good Principles, that now he had no doubt they should agree upon a good Constitution. Governor Martin of North Carolina and for six years a Senator of the United States, who had been a Member of the Convention that formed the Constitution told me, that my "Defence" had produced the Constitution of the United States.

Dr Morse told me, that he was informed from good Authority that my "Defence" had produced an entire Revolution in the Sentiments of the Convention, and influenced the Members to agree to the Constitution that was adopted. I have learned the same Fact from many other Sources."

—John Adams

Mercy's ideas and opinions were so important that even a future President of the United States hated the thought of her disapproving of something he had written and took the time to try to get her to change her mind!

Mercy took a rigid stance against the establishment of the Constitution—a document near and dear to John Adams and many of the Founders. Her dislike for the Constitution came from a place of distrust for central government in general. She was also concerned that there wasn't much in the country's laws about giving women access to a formal and equal education. She recognized that not all women came from families like hers who believed it was just as valuable to educate women as it was to educate men. She had hoped that these great minds would address this issue.

Today, Mercy would be considered a classical liberal. She believed that the protection of a human being's inalienable rights was the most important purpose a government could serve, and that these protections must be at the heart of any free and prosperous society.

Life, Liberty, and the Pursuit of Happiness

The rights to life, liberty, and the freedom to pursue happiness were central principles in the Declaration of Independence. The rights to these, the founders declared, were not up for debate. And Mercy agreed.

Liberty is defined as "the state of being free within society from oppressive restrictions imposed by authority on one's way of life, behavior, or political views." Mercy believed that a government didn't *give* rights to people but that they already had rights from the moment of their birth. To Mercy and others, the job of government was to ensure that people's natural rights were never taken away or made conditional.

The right to life didn't mean that everyone was guaranteed long, happy, or prosperous life—it meant that every human being had the right to exist freely and to live their life as they saw fit so long as they were not causing harm to others. The right to pursue happiness, likewise, didn't mean that everyone was guaranteed happiness, or that it was the government's job to make sure people had what they wanted or needed. It merely meant that the government couldn't stand in the way of a person's right to attempt to build the life they wanted and pursue the things that would make them happy and prosperous.

The exercise of these rights to life, liberty, and the pursuit of happiness must not come at the expense of others' rights to the same. This means that the government can't stand in the way of people pursuing what they think is best for themselves and their families, but that people also cannot exercise their rights in such a way that it prevents others from living their lives and exercising their rights to life, liberty, and the pursuit of happiness as well.

Because of her strong sense of moral right and wrong, Mercy was solidly against slavery and argued that it didn't have a place in the newly founded United States of America. She didn't feel that the Constitution went far enough in protecting the rights of *all* people, and she was consistently critical of anything that fell short of demanding the protection of inalienable rights for everyone. Not until the Bill of Rights was ratified in the winter of 1791 did Mercy begin to feel somewhat comfortable with the government of her new nation.

Throughout her life, Mercy remained steadfast in her beliefs and never hesitated to take pen to paper in fiery criticism of anyone—friend or foe—who failed to adhere to the principles she believed were essential to keep men free. At the age of sixty, when most women were settling into a quiet country life, Mercy published a piece called *Observations on the New Constitution*, expounding on her criticism of an authoritative central government.

She was viewed by all who knew her as a staunch advocate of individual freedom and limited government, and she used her talent as a writer and storyteller to bring other patriots to the cause, drawing the praise of George Washington, John Adams, and other giants of the Revolution. Even though she was often critical of him, Alexander Hamilton, in reference to Mercy, remarked that, "In the career of dramatic composition at least, female genius in the United States has outstripped the male."

Mercy died on October 19, 1814, at the age of 86. She had outlived many of the men who founded the United States, and her contribution to the spirit of America would live on in many of its future leaders. It's easy to imagine John Adams as President, ever mindful—and possibly fearful—of the tongue-lashing he would someday receive if he failed to live up to the expectations of one Mercy Otis Warren.

Aleksandr
SOLZHENITSYN

As an outspoken critic of Communism, Aleksandr helped to raise global awareness of the Soviet Gulag forced-labor camp system and the atrocities of the Soviet Union.

A Critic of Communism

Just days after learning he was going to be a father, Isaa-kiy Solzhenitsyn died tragically in a hunting accident. His son, Aleksandr, would often think about his dad. He liked to imagine what he would look like, what his voice would sound like, and whether he would be proud of the boy he was and the young man he was becoming. When he looked down at his own hands while chopping wood, or holding a pencil, he wondered if his square fingers and wide palms resembled those of the man he only knew through stories.

Aleksandr's mother, Taisiya, was a well-educated woman from a wealthy family, but when her husband died, she was left without much. Her son was born in Kislovodsk, Russia, on a cold morning in December of 1918, and although she never remarried, she had the companionship of her sister throughout the rest of her life. Together, they raised Aleksandr by working hard and making do with the little they had.

Aleksandr's childhood was set largely in the midst of war and upheaval. His young years coincided with the Russian Civil War, fought between the Red Army and Vladamir Lenin, who wanted Bolshevik-style socialism, and the White Army, led by people who wanted capitalism and democracy. Lenin and the Red Army won, and Russia was thrust into communism.

Communism

Under communist rule, the government claimed all prop-erty—even farms and houses—as their own. They said it "belonged to the people," but people who had lived before the Communists took over knew what they really meant.

People like Aleksandr's mom and aunt were still allowed to live in their homes and work on their farms, but they couldn't quit working on their farms—even if they wanted to—and most of what they worked to plant, tend, and harvest was taken by the government and redistributed to others. The Communists said that this was fair.

They told the people that it was moral for each person to produce what they could through hard work, and that the fruits of their labor should then be collected and redistributed to other people who couldn't, or wouldn't, work as hard.

But people quickly learned that whether they worked hard or hardly worked at all, they still got the same food and the same amount of money as everyone else. The communists said that it was fair, but people who remembered life before the war knew that it was wrong.

Because Aleksandr was only a boy when the communists took over his country, and because he was taught in government schools, he grew up believing that the government was right and that communism was good. Even though he saw his sweet mother suffer while working the farm that had once belonged to her and her husband but now belonged to the state—and even though he himself often went without—he still believed what he had been taught in school.

A Forbidden Letter

Aleksandr's mother loved literature and poetry. She loved

to write and read and learn new things, and she passed her passion for beautiful words and lovely thoughts on to her son. When he was a young man, Aleksandr moved off to the city to attend university. He was a good student and studied difficult subjects. He liked to challenge himself.

A few years later, a shadow fell across the world. Adolf Hitler had risen to power, and he and his Nazi army were spreading the work of death across Europe. A man named Joseph Stalin had risen to power in Russia, and he allied the Red Army with the allied forces of the United States, England, and France to stop Hitler. Aleksandr left university and joined the Red Army. He wanted to fight.

While he was serving on the front lines of the war, he saw his fellow soldiers do things that he knew weren't right. He also noticed his government doing things that he didn't think were right. One day, he wrote a letter to his friend Nikolai. In his letter, he said that he didn't think that Stalin was doing a very good job leading Russia anymore, and that he had started to think that the country needed to be organized in a better way.

Aleksandr didn't know that all of the mail that the people of Russia sent to each other was read by the government before it was delivered. When SHMERSH—this was the name for Stalin's secret police force that spied on the people of Russia to make sure that they were loyal to their government—read Aleksandr's words, they immediately sent police to arrest him.

Stalin didn't care that Aleksandr was serving loyally in the Red Army. He wouldn't allow anyone to speak out against the way he was leading the country. Aleksandr was charged with spreading anti-Soviet propaganda and sentenced to eight years of prison in the labor camps of Siberia, which were called gulags. While serving his eight-year prison sentence, he began to write poems and stories in his mind. He often didn't have access to pens and paper, so he would memorize the stories other prisoners told him about their lives and what had happened to them in the gulags.

He memorized long poems about the atrocities he saw committed by his fellow soldiers during the war—he knew that he had to write it all down someday. The world had to know what was happening inside communist Russia.

A Story to Tell

Toward the end of Aleksandr's prison term, Joseph Stalin died, and a man named Nikita Khrushchev came to power. One day, in 1956, Khrushchev stood before the members of the 20th Congress of the Communist Party of the Soviet Union and gave what became known as his "Secret Speech." In his speech, the new leader of Russia gave a detailed account of the atrocities committed by Joseph Stalin. It is estimated that Stalin was responsible for the deaths of over 20 million civilians during his brutal rule, and Khrushchev was the first person to speak openly about it.

Under Khrushchev's leadership, Aleksandr was freed and allowed to return home to start his new life. He took a job as a teacher during the day, but he spent all of his nights writing all the things he had tucked away and memorized during his years in the gulags.

In 1962, at the age of 44, he published *1962: One Day in the Life of Ivan Denisovich*, a fictional novel about life under Stalinist rule. Unlike years earlier, when Aleksandr was sent to prison camps for questioning his government, those now in power praised his work and even helped him to get it published. Nikita Khrushchev believed Aleksandr's book was important because, he said, "There's a Stalinist in each of you; there's even a Stalinist in me. We must root out this evil."

Aleksandr's book was even studied in schools across all of Russia.

The Gulag Archipelago

In 1964, Khrushchev was removed from power, and life in Russia became less free again. Aleksandr again began to worry that his writing would get him in trouble. Eventually, under heavy persecution, he moved to Germany and, later, to the United States. In 1973, Aleksandr published *The Gulag Archipelago*—a three-volume, seven-part work about the Soviet prison system. He wrote from his own experiences as well as the accounts of more than 250 of his fellow prisoners, creating a detailed and harrowing picture of life inside communist Russia and its infamous gulags.

The Gulag Archipelago is considered one of the most influential books of the twentieth century and has sold over 30 million copies and been translated into 35 languages.

Toward the end of his life, Aleksandr looked back on all that he had lived through, reflecting on all that he had done. He said,

Over a half century ago, while I was still a child, I recall hearing a number of old people offer the following explanation for the great disasters that had befallen Russia: "Men have forgotten God; that's why all this has happened." Since then I have spent well-nigh 50 years working on the history of our revolution; in the process I have read hundreds of books, collected hundreds of personal testimonies, and have already contributed eight volumes of my own toward the effort of clearing away the rubble left by that upheaval. But if I were asked today to formulate as concisely as possible the main cause of the ruinous revolution that swallowed up some 60 million of our people, I could not put it more accurately than to repeat: "Men have forgotten God; that's why all this has happened.

Aleksandr Solzhenitsyn was finally able to return home to Russia in 1994, after having spent nearly two decades in the United States. He died at the age of 89, and his funeral was attended by Russian heads of state and world leaders who recognized the contributions and sacrifices he had made to bring the horrors of Marxism to light and warn the world of what could happen when men and women were not permitted to live, worship, and work in their own way.

His life and all that he taught us can be summed up in his own words:

> What about the main thing in life, all its riddles? If you want, I'll spell it out for you right now. Do not pursue what is illusionary—property and position... Rub your eyes and purify your heart—and prize above all else in the world those who love you and who wish you well.

So, what did you think?

Are you ready to stand up for what's right in the crazy world around us? Can you take courage like these heroes and champion a good cause?

We're not sure what that looks like for us quite yet—like you, we're still young. But our parents have taught us a lot so that we'll be ready for the world and able to defend what we believe against the many voices who disagree and support bad ideas.

A lot of important progress has been made in the world because of these heroes, and we want to help make the world an even better place. So we're hoping that we can be inspired by these stories, and others like them, so that if and when we're in a situation that calls for it, we can also stand up for what's right and set an example for others.

We hope you feel inspired to do the same!

—The Tuttle Twins